Reading the Movies

Reading the Movies

Twelve Great Films on Video
and How to Teach Them

William V. Costanzo
Westchester Community College

National Council of Teachers of English
1111 Kenyon Road, Urbana, Illinois 61801

To my children, Michael and David, who taught me enough about reading movies to write a book.

Film photos: Museum of Modern Art/Film Stills Archive. Courtesy of Columbia Pictures (*On the Waterfront, Mr. Smith Goes to Washington, Awakenings*); Embassy Pictures (*The Graduate*); MGM (*Singin' in the Rain*); Orca Productions, Sunafra Productions, and NEF Diffusion (*Sugar Cane Alley*); RKO Pictures (*Citizen Kane*); Twentieth Century-Fox (*The Grapes of Wrath*); United Artists (*Modern Times*); Universal Pictures (*The Birds, Do the Right Thing*); and Warner Brothers (*Rebel Without a Cause*). William Costanzo's photograph courtesy of Dale Leifeste Photography, Valhalla, New York.

Manuscript Editor: Mary Daniels

Production Editor: Rona S. Smith

Cover Design and Illustration: Carlton Bruett

Interior Design: Tom Kovacs for TGK Design

NCTE Stock Number 39108-3050

Library of Congress Cataloging-in-Publication Data

Costanzo, William V.
    Reading the movies : twelve great films on video and how to teach them / William V. Costanzo.
       p.   cm.
    Includes bibliographical references.
    Includes filmographies.
    ISBN 0-8141-3910-8
    1. Motion pictures—Study and teaching. 2. Motion pictures and literature. 3. Motion pictures—Philosophy. 4. Film criticism.
I. Title.
PN1993.7.C6 1991
791.43'07—dc20   91-40981
                                                CIP

Contents

Acknowledgements

The idea for this book was first suggested by Charles Suhor, NCTE's farsighted deputy director and a long-time advocate of media education. Charlie believed that the day had arrived to publish a guidebook on film for teachers of English. I was quick to seize the day. Such a book had been ripening in my imagination through years of teaching film and trading classroom stories with enthusiastic colleagues. If there were space enough and time, I would list each student, friend, and colleague who has contributed to the contents of this volume. There are some, however, to whom I owe an especially large measure of appreciation. In particular, I want to thank Bruce Kawin (University of Colorado, Boulder) and Peter Brunette (George Mason University) for reading portions of the manuscript with an expert and judicious eye. Their scholarship and friendship have helped to shape this book and sustain the spirit of its author. I want to thank Linda Dittmar (University of Massachusetts–Boston) and Ernece Kelly (Kingsborough Community College, New York) for helping with the selection of films. Their perspectives have enlarged my view of movies as well as the scope of this text. To Barbra Morris (University of Michigan, Ann Arbor), Jonathan Lovell (San Jose State University), and my other associates on the Media Commission, I owe many years of supportive and productive collaboration. And I thank my good fortune in having Michael Spooner, NCTE's senior editor for publications, and Mary Daniels, my patient and film-wise copy editor, to guide me through the publication process with high hopes and unflagging patience.

I work at a school that takes great pride in teaching but also supports the efforts of its teachers to strengthen the bonds with and within their professions through scholarship and publication. The productive climate of Westchester Community College is due largely to its energetic president, Joseph N. Hankin, and to its extraordinary staff. As always, I am grateful to my generous colleagues in the WCC library who helped provide the resources for my work and then made sure that I sat down to do it. I am grateful, too, for the advice of teachers like Stanley Feingold, John Cuniberti, and Maryanne Vent, who helped to show me the range of possibilities while keeping me faithful to my own.

Finally, a note of personal appreciation to my family: to my parents for their belief in me, to my children for keeping me alert, and to my wife, Barbara, for standing by me through the years.

Preface

The wave of enthusiasm for film study that crested in the early 1970s, then ebbed during the back-to-basics movement of the following decade, has begun to rise again, impelled by advances in research and technology. With the advent of VCRs, movies have become more popular, less costly, and easier to screen. Not only are movies more accessible than ever before, but laserdisk and videocassette machines also have made it possible to give films the close textual attention once reserved for literary works. Meanwhile, new scholarship in fields like semiotics, post-structuralism, and feminist studies has added fresh significance and sophistication to the analysis of moving images. Film is more widely seen now as a symbol system, much like language, which encodes the values of society, reflecting and reforming our most essential cultural beliefs.

For these and other reasons, the idea of using movies is growing more attractive—and important—to teachers of English. Many English teachers regard film as part of the linguistic environment. They recognize that much of what their students learn about language and culture is filtered through the visual media. They seek to make more natural and substantive the connections between the media arts and the language arts.

It seems especially important, then, that teachers have good models and reliable resources for introducing films in the classroom. The purpose of this book is to help teachers develop their own informed approaches to teaching films of high quality and wide appeal. It begins with a general overview of film theory and research, followed by a closer look at twelve specific films, each accompanied by practical ideas for presenting them to students. One of my goals has been to build on what teachers already know, moving beyond the strictly literary categories of text analysis (plot, theme, character, and so on) to cinematic concepts, such as framing, lighting, editing, and sound, without getting too technical. The reader is invited to see correspondences and contrasts between composing and filmmaking, literature and narrative film, reader response and viewer response, trends in literary theory and film criticism. Throughout, I have been guided by a balance of concerns. Without losing sight of the day-to-day realities of classroom teaching, I have sought to steer a steady course between aesthetics and technology, cognitive skills and cultural values, and theory and practice. I hope you find the way inviting.

Introduction: Films, Lives, and Videotape

What if all the motion pictures ever made were suddenly to disappear? What would we have lost? There would be no trace of *Star Wars* (1977), *Gone with the Wind* (1939), or *It's a Wonderful Life* (1946). No Little Tramp, no Humphrey Bogart, Bette Davis, Mickey Mouse. If, along with the films themselves, all recollection of them vanished too, we would have no mental images of Gene Kelly singin' in the rain, of King Kong astride the Empire State Building, of Dustin Hoffman outfitted after graduation in a wet suit, of Gary Cooper walking down a dusty western street at high noon. A good portion of our collective visual memory would have disappeared.

More than pictures would be lost. We would probably have to expunge from our vocabulary words like *close-up, freeze-frame, reverse angle, fade-out,* and *out of sync,* along with the perceptual habits they refer to. Gone with the films would be the countless ways in which they have trained us to observe the world. Without the model of the movies, much of our mental editing, focusing, and filtering would be unthinkable.

Beyond the stories, images, and cinematic methods, there is the industry itself. What if all the people, places, and things associated with the movies were to vanish too? Imagine no more movie theaters, film distributors, studios, or video rental stores. A huge chunk would be gouged out of the national economy. So would a large portion of the working population. Gone would be the screen stars, writers, film directors, camera operators, sound technicians, gaffers, and gofers who populate the movie world. Gone would be their cameras, editing machines, projectors, props—the tools of the trade that make it possible to mass-produce those animated stories for a mass audience.

Beyond the stories, too, are the issues they illuminate. Consider how *I Am a Fugitive from a Chain Gang* (1932) focused national attention on prison reform during the thirties, how the "Why We Fight" series (1943–45) contributed to the war effort during the forties, how films like *Rebel Without a Cause* (1955) highlighted the problems of alienated youth during the fifties. More recent films have raised contemporary issues to new levels of awareness, among them *Roger and Me* (1989),

1

Stand and Deliver (1987), *Born on the Fourth of July* (1990), and *Do the Right Thing* (1989). For decades, movies have projected the concerns of every generation on the nation's screen of consciousness. What would our shared view of world events be like without them?

Then there is the film experience itself, the feeling of being pulled into another world, a place of deferred resistance or suspended disbelief where we can be, for a little while, in someone else's skin, on intimate terms with the unfamiliar, or face-to-face with our own repressed desires. What is this experience that we would lose if it were never possible to have "lost it at the movies"?

The Need to Study Film

Somewhere in this vision of a world without motion pictures are good reasons for studying film. Since their invention nearly a century ago, movies have become a significant component of our culture, part of our individual and collective lives. Something of this magnitude demands careful, serious attention, as many teachers, particularly teachers of English, have come to recognize.

"We live in a total-information culture, which is being increasingly dominated by the image," observed John Culkin more than two decades ago. "Intelligent living within such an environment calls for developing habits of perception, analysis, judgment, and selectivity that are capable of processing the relentless input of visual data." Culkin called on the schools to shape these habits. "Schools are where the tribe passes on its values to the young. Schools are where film study should take place" (Schillaci 1970, 19). In Chicago, Ralph Amelio has taken this challenge to heart. The goal of his film program at Willowbrook High School is "to develop in the student the habits of analysis, criticism, understanding, and appreciation of film in a disciplined and creative manner." Amelio links this goal to the humanistic education of his students, "to gain insight and aesthetic enjoyment of [their] own experience and of others through film" (1971, 7). At the University of Iowa, Dudley Andrew applies a similar belief within a college setting. To Andrew, "films are cultural objects to be mastered and experiences that continually master us." "Education," he believes, "is best served by a dialectic that forces us to interrogate films and then to interrogate ourselves in front of films" (Grant 1983, 43–44). This philosophy is supported by NCTE's Commission on Media, which broadens the definition of literacy (and therefore the mission of all English teachers) to include film and other media. In its "Rationale for Integrating Media into English and the Language Arts," the Commission affirms that "teaching students to discover meaning and to communicate effectively now requires knowing how electronic media function in the development of language, thought, and knowledge in our culture" (1983, 1).

Many students already recognize this need as an irrefutable fact of life. From a survey which I give my students every term, I have been astonished to learn that they are now watching an average of twenty-two films per month. They watch films on broadcast television, on cable networks, on videocassettes, and in the local theaters. It's not unusual to spend an evening with friends watching a double feature on the family VCR or to chain-view several movies at the multiplex. Why do they want to study film? Why devote school time to the movies when films are everywhere? My students are fascinated by the pull of motion pictures. "I can forget it's not real sometimes," they say. "I get swept away." They want to understand what lies behind their own attraction to the screen. Many are curious about the creative work that goes into a movie. They want to learn how films are made, how they're "put together," what goes on behind the camera and beyond the screen. A few have tried their hand at acting or photography; they are interested in learning more about the people who make films. Nearly all want to be more knowledgeable viewers, to know about the history, the technology, the art, the craft, the principles that drive the films they love to watch.

These are favorable times, then, to bring movies into the mainstream of education, to make film study part of the ongoing curriculum. There has never been a clearer rationale, a more convincing theoretical framework, or a stronger factual foundation on which to build. What's more, recent advances in technology have made the study of film more practical, more practicable than ever before. Anyone with a VCR or videodisk player now has access to the same film titles that were available to a few privileged libraries and universities only several years ago. Furthermore, by pressing a few buttons on a standard remote-control device, any teacher or student can perform feats of film analysis that used to require costly, intricate equipment using fragile 16mm film.

The Video Revolution

The VCR and its kindred technologies are revolutionizing the movies. Videocassette recorders are much simpler to operate than projectors. Videocassettes are easier to carry, less expensive, and more readily available than reels of film. As a result, the technology has changed not only the way we watch and study movies, but also the film industry itself.

Movies are becoming more like books. A videocassette can fit into your book bag or be stored on any bookshelf. This means that the film version of *To Kill a Mockingbird* (1962) can sit next to the novel in your literature collection or be carried to class along with the book. Students and their teachers can lend each other copies of Laurence Olivier's *Hamlet* (1948) or Roman Polanski's *Macbeth* (1971) as readily as trading copies of the printed plays. My own students often hand in film-study assignments with a cassette already cued to the pertinent scene.

As videocassettes become more accessible, their numbers grow more plentiful. Film titles have proliferated in video rental shops, retail stores, and libraries, as well as supermarkets. People now scan the shelves for a promising film title as they would for a good book. At home, they sometimes watch the video with habits carried over from their reading. They might replay a compelling scene, skip over tedious sections of the story, or save their place at any point. The scan, fast-forward, freeze, and electronic bookmark features of the VCR give users nearly as much control over their viewing as they have over their reading.

What does all this mean for the current and future status of film? First, more people are watching more movies. Most homes now have at least one VCR. Videocassette sales and rentals have become multi-billion-dollar industries. With some 50,000 titles to choose from, Americans have more options than ever before. While not every title is a movie classic, the increasing availability of films has made viewers more conscious of the classics, and it has made the classics easier to see. As people become more experienced viewers, they become curious about the history of film; they want to see earlier examples of their favorite genres and watch other movies featuring their favorite stars or made by the same directors. They are more interested in trying other kinds of film. The more they watch, the more knowledgeable viewers become. The nation is becoming more film literate.

This, in turn, creates a larger market for movies. The early fears that videocassettes would siphon off audiences from the theaters have proved ill-founded. In fact, the opposite has happened. Increased revenues from videocassettes enable film producers to make more movies and rebuild the theater-going audience. According to Vincent Canby, "the videocassette recorder has been the greatest boon to theatrical films since the refinement of sound" (1989, 19). This trend has been particularly kind to early films. Film distributors who once were reluctant to bother with old movies now are willing to look for the best available prints and invest in their restoration. On the whole, the movie industry is healthier today than it was just before video-cassettes arrived on the scene.

The VCR Experience

In addition to its influence on audience viewing habits and the film industry, the VCR is changing the experience of watching films. Part of this experience is technological, part may be physiological, and part is social and environmental.

Current video technology requires that the large-screen image of the theater be shrunk to the proportions of television, thus reducing picture quality. Some of the picture must be sacrificed when the rectangular dimensions of the wide screen are clipped to fit the box-like video screen. Photographic values are also lost. The range of contrast between the brightest and darkest shades of an optical (film) image can be as high as 100 to 1. In an electronic (video) image, the ratio is only 20 to 1. This means that the video version of a movie has only one-fifth as much contrast as the original film (Fantel 1990a, 32). Along with these gradations of detail, much of the rich color and three-dimensional effect of deep-focus photography is diminished in the smaller frame. This is particularly true of those larger-than-life films like *Citizen Kane* (1941) and *Lawrence of Arabia* (1962). Their sense of space and subtlety of tone tend to be eclipsed by dialogue and story. Since what survives best is the script, Joseph Mankiewicz and Woody Allen translate better than Orson Welles and David Lean. Aesthetic values which depend on technological factors may, however, change with the technology. As high-resolution forms of video are developed, both screen size and picture quality may increase to the point where electronic versions are equal or superior to optical prints (Fantel, 1990b).

The distinctions between electronic and optical projection, however, may go beyond technology. Dimitri Balachoff believes that there are physiological differences. After observing people watch hundreds of movies over a span of fifteen years, he concludes that there may be shifts in perception and cognition. In optical projection, twenty-four complete images are projected every second. In electronic projection, the image is refreshed by 400,000 individual points of light per second. The optical image is replaced holistically; the electronic image is replaced sequentially, bit by bit. This may mean that the two kinds of image are processed differently in the brain. Balachoff associates the optical image with the "synergistic, rhythmic, and harmonic" functions of the right cerebral hemisphere. He associates the electronic image with "punctual, sequential, and analytic" operations of the left hemisphere. Arguing that "the subject of film is not the essence of it," Balachoff concludes that the video screen cannot transmit the "latent content, the hidden meaning that gives a film its real value" (1989, 55).

There is more to watching movies than just the images and sounds, however they are produced. There is also the social and environmental context. Compare the experience of sitting in a darkened theater with a group of strangers, concentrating on the screen, to the experience at home, where the surroundings are familiar, the lights are likely to be on, and attention is diverted by innumerable distractions. Going out to the movies makes the act of viewing a more focused event. A larger audience tends to magnify the experience; it multiplies the laughter and the tears. Furthermore, when a movie is projected on the screen, it seems to have its own momentum. Without a remote-control device to tinker with the sound or speed, it's easier to be swept along. Nonetheless, advances in videodisk technology have increased the popularity of videos and their usefulness in the classroom.

Video in the Classroom

Nearly seven million videodisks were sold in 1990 (Fantel, 1990b). These disks, which store images and sound in digital form, are less expensive than videocassettes and produce sharper, denser pictures. They can also be controlled more precisely. With a videodisk version of *Citizen Kane*, the viewer can jump instantly to any frame of any scene and hold the image for any length of time. Dual sound tracks make it possible to shift back and forth, say, between the original dialogue of a French film and a dubbed, English translation, or between the primary track and a narrator commenting on each scene. Moreover, videodisks can be controlled by a computer, so that students can work interactively with images, sound, and textual information in a multimedia environment. Such options make videodisks excellent tools for film analysis.

All this may seem both bewitching and bewildering to teachers of English who are concerned about preparation, curricular priorities, and time. Their uneasiness can be heard in the faculty lounge: "I'm an

English teacher, not a media specialist. I know that movies have this power, but I have no special training to teach them. Most of my students know more than I do about films." "My main business is with reading, writing, listening, and speaking; I just don't have much time for showing movies." "Yes, I know that many of my kids prefer to watch the movie than to read the book, but what can I do about it?" "Actually, I feel a little guilty if we're having fun."

This book is partly a response to voices such as these. It will not answer all the arguments or allay all the anxieties, but for those who recognize the importance of film in their students' lives and want to acknowledge this importance in their classrooms—actively, productively, significantly—this book is offered as a resource and a guide.

Organization of the Book

I have divided the book into two parts. Each chapter in Part One takes up an area of film study that has been productively explored by scholars and offers rewarding opportunities for further exploration by students and teachers. Chapter 1 adopts the aesthetic view. It considers filmmaking as an art, especially an art of storytelling, comparing literary narratives to cinematic narratives, as well as film's relationship to the other arts. Chapter 2 traces the codes and conventions which enable us to understand a film. Drawing on research in semiotics and viewer response, this chapter considers the degree to which watching movies is a natural or a learned behavior and the degree to which cinema constitutes a language or symbol system. In so doing, it clarifies the place of film study among the language arts. The technical side of film production—the machinery behind the movies and the people behind the machines—is discussed in Chapter 3, while Chapter 4 gives a concise chronology of film from its beginnings to the present, identifying major trends and variations. Chapter 5 introduces some of the most influential and illuminating thoughts on the nature of cinema and its place in our culture and our private lives. Concluding the first section is Chapter 6, which gives an overview of film study in the profession, including pedagogical trends, different approaches, classroom methods, activities, assignments, and issues of censorship and copyright.

Part Two focuses on twelve films that have proved successful in the classroom. For each film, I have included screen credits, cast listings, background information, discussion questions, topics for further study, and suggested films and readings. In selecting these films, I found it difficult to be fully representative. The list does span a range of periods and styles (Charlie Chaplin to Spike Lee), genres (musical, horror, comedy), and themes (growing up, society and individuality, the American Dream), but there are inevitable omissions and some uneasy proportions. There are no silent films, for example, or documentaries, there is only one foreign-language film, two films directed by women, and two directed by blacks. For the most part, I have chosen mainstream American feature films—all screened in class with favorable results—under the assumption that readers will make their own selection and supplement these films to suit their students and objectives.

Let me explain my choices. I emphasize feature films because they are closer to the content of most English courses than are documentaries or experimental films. Because they tell a story, feature films can be read as literature. I emphasize American films because they are more readily available and easier to read than foreign films, both culturally and literally. Students who have seen few foreign-language films often are distracted by the subtitles, especially on a small screen. That doesn't mean our students ought to go through life as cinematic xenophobes; a judicious introduction to films from other countries can open their eyes to worlds beyond the American screen. Though most of the twelve films in Part Two are movie classics, I have also selected a few more recent works.

Initially, my students are as resistant to black-and-white photography as they are to literary classics, but they often thank me for introducing them to Charlie Chaplin, Katherine Hepburn, Clark Gable, and other "old-time greats." Once they get used to the idea of watching movies made before 1980, once past the barrier of unfamiliarity, they even seek more classics on their own. Yet a course based entirely on the traditional film canon would have disadvantages. There is the issue of value, for example. What makes a movie great? Who decides when a film becomes a classic? By including recent films that have not yet stood the test of time, we give students the chance to evaluate movies before telling them they have been watching an acknowledged masterpiece or a fleeting fad. Then there are issues of authorship and representation. The sexual and racial history of Hollywood and of the nation has included few women or minority directors. With a few exceptions, it is only in the last decade or so that filmmakers like Euzhan Palcy, Spike Lee, and Penny Marshall have had access to the means of film production for a large audience. I have selected *Sugar Cane Alley, Do the Right Thing,* and *Awakenings*—all made within the last ten years—partly to restore some balance to the classical canon. But I have also included them because, with my students, I believe them to be well-made films about important subjects. Fortunately, the videocassette has reduced the span between a film's appearance and its availability for study. No longer do schools have to wait ten years to buy a 16mm print, then keep it for another twenty to justify the cost. Our film libraries need not smell like mausoleums.

My list of twelve great films, then, is only one of many possibilities. The list of "More Great Films" (Appendix 1) offers some alternatives, while Appendix 2 offers some specific projects. Your readings, your students, and your film experiences will give you still more options. And that is what I've aimed for. If this book encourages you to create your own film course, or to introduce films in your classes with greater confidence, awareness, and success, it will have served its purpose.

I Reading the Movies

1 The Art of Fiction Film

Why see the movie if you've read the book? Why read the book if you've already seen the movie? One reason such questions keep coming up lies in the extraordinary number of movies that are based on literature. John Harrington estimates that one-third of all films ever made are derived from novels (1977, 117). If we add other literary forms, such as drama and short stories, the estimates increase to sixty-five percent or more. We know that a movie like *A Passage to India* (1984) can reach a greater audience in a few weeks than the book has enjoyed since it was published. We also know that a successful movie adaptation can catapult a book high up on the bestseller list.

Beyond questions of numbers, the practice of comparing literature and film raises deeper issues about literacy, contrasting media, and the purposes of art. Consider these statements made by students in a freshman literature class which includes the study of both literature and film:

> In high school, when I read *To Kill a Mockingbird*, I kept getting distracted. I couldn't get the full meaning of the book. Then I borrowed the videotape and watched it with some friends. That's when I really enjoyed and understood the story.

> Film lets you see pictures of what's going on. I got more out of watching *Julius Caesar* than out of reading just the words.

> Literature provides more stimulation than movies. In a film, it's all provided for you. When I saw *Lord of the Flies*, I was disappointed in the characters.

> Film can use things like lighting and sound to create effects that are not really possible in literature. It was hard for me to follow the scene changes when I read *Death of a Salesman*, but I could see [them] clearly in the movie.

> Film can distort the story in translating it to the screen. Young children may never learn to read if we show movies instead of giving them books.

> Film is another form of storytelling.

> Film should be taught as film.

> Film and literature should go hand in hand.

Teachers of English will recognize the seeds of a debate here, the first steps of an inquiry into the nature of narrative and our universal need for stories. What do we look for in a story? What do literary texts and fiction films deliver? What are the common elements and differences in their delivery? What does it mean to be "faithful to the book"? How have literature and film influenced each other? How are they related to music, architecture, dance, and the other arts?

The Art of Storytelling

We are dealing here with films and books that narrate stories. Scholars like Seymour Chatman (1978) use the term *narratology* to emphasize the shared features of storytelling, no matter what the medium may be: a speech, a written text, a movie, or a dance. In the history of narrative, film is a latecomer: Homer's epics date back to about 800 B.C., the novel is generally said to have begun in the eighteenth century, the short story in the early nineteenth century, but movies have been around only since the 1890s. Yet we know that each new narrative form derives from earlier traditions. *The Odyssey* and *Beowulf* can be traced to stories developed and preserved through earlier oral forms. The novel has its origins in the Renaissance novella, the medieval romance, and even works of classical antiquity, like *The Satyricon.* The short-story form reaches back to folklore, myth, fables, and parables. So it should not surprise us that film, too, draws on earlier strategies and structures of narration.

Chatman distinguishes between story and discourse, the "what" and the "how" of narrative. He identifies story with plot, character, setting, and the other elements which critics have traditionally ascribed to a story's "content." He identifies discourse with the means by which a story is communicated. From this point of view, a novel and a film may share the same story, say of Anna Karenina, but they may vary widely in their literary or cinematic forms of discourse. The novel represents the character of Anna in printed words, through dialogue, description, interior monologue, and the author's comments. The film represents Anna in sound and moving images: the gestures, face, and voice of Greta Garbo complemented by the conventions of music, sound effects, costumes, sets, camera work, and a supporting cast.

Our perceptions of Anna depend partly on our understanding of literary, cinematic, and socially constructed codes. As viewers, we know that Anna is in love with Vronsky by the light in Garbo's eyes and the warmth in her voice. We also know this from the camera's lingering close-ups and the music swelling through the sound track. We have learned to read these signs by watching people and from watching films. As readers, in a sense, we have less work to do because Tolstoy interprets Anna's face for us. His description makes us see the flash in her eyes, the brimming smile. At one point, he simply tells us she's in love.

Our understanding of character also depends on another element of narrative: point of view. A novel or short story may be related from varying perspectives, ranging from omniscient to restricted, objective to subjective, and authoritative to unreliable. As readers, we learn to weigh information according to its source, so we look for clues about the story's point of view. We look for contradictions between the author and the authorial voice, between dialogue and monologue, between speech and action. In John Cheever's story, "The Swimmer," bits of overheard conversation and references to changing seasons hint that the story is being told from the protagonist's subjective and increasingly questionable perspective, that the events take place over a period of years, not in a single day. The movie version (1968) follows the same unreliable point of view, but viewers tend to take each event as an objective fact because the discourse of film is more literal-minded. So strong is the illusion of reality in movies that filmmakers have developed a set of codes to indicate subjective points of view. Ingmar Bergman uses a distorting lens to represent Professor Borg's dreams in *Wild Strawberries* (1957). Tony Richardson uses freeze-frames in *The Loneliness of the Long Distance Runner* (1962) to show flashes of the runner's past. Robert Enrico uses slow motion and special sound effects in *An Occurrence at Owl Creek Bridge* (1962) as clues that we are witnessing events in Farquhar's imagination, not reality. Similar distinctions can be made about the use of setting, symbolism, plot, or tone. These elements are common to both written and filmed fiction, but they are developed quite differently within the discourse of each medium.

The Elements of Film Discourse

In some ways, cinematic discourse may seem richer than literary discourse. Films appeal more directly to the eye and ear. True, written language has a visual form and can be read aloud, but the foundering of a ship and the howling of the wind must be evoked by words in the reader's imagination, whereas they can be recreated in light and sound for the film audience. To verbal language, film adds the languages of color, movement, music, and natural and artificial sounds. To the linguistic conventions of diction and syntax, film adds principles of framing, lighting, editing, visual transitions, and montage. This is not to say that film is somehow superior to literature; on the contrary, it is often argued that literary codes are far more precise and elaborately developed than those of film. The point is simply that film covers a wider range of direct sensory experience. Consider just a few of the filmmaker's tools:

Lighting. Etymologists like to remind us that the word *photography* means "writing with light." The language of lighting has its own vocabulary, which viewers learn partly by attending to the visual texts of films. As Bernard Dick observes, "lighting can express subtleties of character, plot, and setting" (1978, 7). High-key lighting, in which most of the scene is brightly lit, produces a buoyant mood, as in the party scene of *Citizen Kane*. Low-key lighting, in which less illumination produces deep contrasts, gives an eerie, ominous feeling to moments like Kane's deathbed scene. Front lighting softens a face, giving it the look of innocence. Bottom lighting makes a face look sinister by casting shadows on the upper lip and hollowing the eyes. Such effects control the connotations of a scene, creating fine shades of emotional meaning. Lighting can be symbolic, too. When the reporter in *Citizen Kane* speaks of searching for the meaning of Rosebud, his face is obscured in shadow. Literally and figuratively, he is in the dark.

Color. Filmmakers use the social codes of color to develop character and mood. In *The Graduate* (1967), the seductive Mrs. Robinson appears in stark shades of red or black, while her ingenuous daughter dresses in soft pinks. The whites and ice-blue tones of Ben's suburban home reaffirm the cold sterility of his parents' world. In *Rebel Without a Cause* (1955), Jim's red jacket and Judy's red coat link them to each other and isolate them from the adults who fail to heed their cries for help. My students have little trouble noticing these cues once they recognize the signficance of color in our lives, but they sometimes ask how deliberately a filmmaker selects the colors for a set. They are often intrigued to learn that Michelangelo Antonioni repainted the bedroom set of *Red Desert* (1964) so that it changed from white to red after the lovemaking scene, and that he spray-painted an entire marsh a certain shade of grey in order to reflect the mood of his characters in that scene.

Framing. The four edges of the movie screen frame the camera's field of vision, our window on the events of any story. We see only what the camera lets us see, through whatever lens is used, from whatever angle is selected. As viewers, our interpretation of setting, character, and action often depends on deliberate placements of the camera. As an example, take the Colorado sequence in *Citizen Kane*. It opens with a long shot of a boy playing in the snow. Then the camera pulls back, revealing that we have been watching him through a window from his mother's point of view. She is inside a cabin, her figure to the left side of the window, calling, "Be careful Charles. Pull your muffler 'round your neck." Next we hear a man's voice, which becomes more distinct as the camera pulls back even farther into the cabin to show the figure of a well-dressed gentleman on the right. Charles's mother says, "I'll sign those papers now, Mr. Thatcher," and moves to the center of the frame, obscuring our view of the window and her son. Now a third figure appears in the cabin, squeezed against the left side of the frame. He says, "You people seem to forget that I'm the boy's father." When the camera finally comes to rest, all four figures are in view: Mrs. Kane and Mr. Thatcher seated at a table in the foreground, the legal papers spread before them; the husband standing on the left, in the middle ground, partly off screen; the boy, a tiny figure in the background, glimpsed through the window in the center of the frame. Even without the dialogue we would understand these personal relationships from the framing. Later, outside the cabin, when Charles learns that he is being sent away, the configuration changes (see Figure 1). Charles and Mrs. Kane dominate the front and center of the frame, Mr. Thatcher looms large but half-obscured by the left edge of the screen, and the father wavers in the background. Now the main interest is between mother and son; the banker's threat and the father's insignificance are represented by their position in the frame.

Motion. Tolstoy was fascinated by this feature of the movies. "The cinema has divined the mystery of motion," he said, "and that is its greatness. It is closer to life" (Harrington 1977, 211). Cinema has produced a language of motion which often speaks louder and more precisely than words. It is Marlon Brando's gestures, not his speech, that reveal most about the character of Terry Malloy in *On the Waterfront* (1954). A quick jerk of the head or a tugging at his nose tell all we need to know about his history as a boxer or his embarrassed sensitivity to Edie Doyle.

Film's movements can be broad as well as slight. When the camera sweeps slowly over Kane's accumulated wealth at the end of *Citizen Kane*, we recognize the emptiness of his career. In another scene, when the camera climbs up to the roof of Susan Alexander's nightclub and

Figure 1. Understanding personal relationships through framing: young Kane meets Mr. Thatcher.

swoops down through the skylight to reveal her figure slumped over a table, we feel it as an intrusion into one of the world's small, broken lives.

Sound. Films reproduce sounds where books can only describe them. Music, dialogue, voice-over (words that are not synchronous with the actors' lips), and natural sounds (sound effects) can contribute not only to a movie's realism, but also to the story's plot, characterization, or symbolism. The sirens that begin and end *Rebel Without a Cause* (1955) are part of the story line—the police are on the way—and also part of the film's symbolic structure, a metaphor for the anguished cry of help. In *The Birds* (1963), Hitchcock makes similar use of bird sounds. When Melanie crosses the street to the pet store, someone gives a bird whistle. In the store, she asks for a talking bird. Later on, the screech of gulls and the whirring of their wings take on ominous significance. These sounds are genuinely chilling, and they seem all the more threatening when we do not see the birds themselves. But what is most terrifying is the absence of sound, when we can neither see nor hear the threat.

Transitions. The simplest transition from one shot to another is the cut, produced by splicing together two pieces of film. Filmmakers soon learned to use special effects—fade-outs, iris-outs, dissolves—to move more deliberately between shots or scenes. To some extent, these optical transitions have come to represent predictable relationships. A dissolve may signify a shift in time or place; a fade may close the shade on a suggestive scene. Cinematic transitions have not become as standardized as punctuation marks, but they do represent a kind of code. Bordwell and Thompson (1986) have catalogued some of Welles's ingenious uses of transitions in *Citizen Kane* (8–23). To contrast the happiness of Kane's Colorado childhood with the dreary circumstances of his adolescence in New York, Welles dissolves from the image of Kane's sled, left behind in the snow, to another sled, a gift from his legal guardian. The white wrapping paper looks like a poor substitute for snow, especially in his new surroundings, a cramped Manhattan apartment where the boy is flanked by solemn servants who intone, "Happy Birthday, Charles." Welles bridges another gap in time, between Kane's first meeting with Susan Alexander and his political career, with a transition of sound. The applause Kane gives to Susan for her singing turns into the ovation for his campaign speech, a campaign which will end abruptly when his affair with Susan is disclosed. Bordwell and Thompson note that the slow dissolves which link together the shots of Kane's estate suggest stagnation and decay. They point out that the transitions that join each scene in the breakfast montage of Kane's first marriage are swish pans, swift camera movements that lead from one scene to the next. The blur of each transition matches the tempo of a waltz theme on the sound track, which grows more dissonant as the marriage breaks down. As viewers, we learn to read such transitional devices as clues, even statements, about relationships within the film.

Adaptation: Questions of Fidelity

Alain Resnais once compared cinematic adaptations to a reheated meal (Beja 1979a, 79). Why rehash the book when you can serve up original films about original stories? Aside from aesthetic reasons, there are clear economic motives for producing adaptations. First, a book offers a ready-made plot. There's no need to develop an untested script. Second, since published books already have an audience, much of the publicity comes free. Third, for all the critical complaints that "the book was better," three out of four Academy Awards for Best Picture have gone to adaptations. And the majority of top-grossing films are adaptations (Beja 1979a, 78). No wonder that most bestselling novels are turned into films. But what about the artistic side? What should we expect of cinematic adaptations? What does it mean to be faithful to the book?

George Bluestone was one of the first to study in depth the phenomenon of adaptations and is still one of the most illuminating writers on the subject. Bluestone sees the filmmaker as an independent artist, "not a translator for an established author, but a new author in his own right" (1957, 62). He points out that many film adapters never read the book, but get their stories from summaries. What they adapt is a kind of paraphrase, "characters and incidents that have detached themselves from language" (1957, 63). Bluestone reminds us that some stories are better suited to one medium than another because "what is peculiarly filmic and what is peculiarly novelistic cannot be converted without destroying an integral part of each" (1957, 63). Joyce and Proust, he concludes, would seem as pointless on screen as Chaplin would in print.

Bluestone would agree with the French director René Clair, who once said, "a faithful translation is often a betrayal of the original" (Harrington 1977, 3). Clair believed that a filmmaker must refashion the substance of the story—its plot, characters, settings, themes—using the tools of cinema, not merely copying the finished artifact produced by the writer's tools. A literal translation would be as foolish as constructing log cabins out of concrete cylinders.

A good example of translating the spirit rather than the letter of a book is Tony Richardson's adaptation of *Tom Jones* (1963). The film opens with a parody of silent movies. The old-fashioned harpsichord music, subtitles, iris shots, and overstated style of acting help to set a comic tone. The sequence also does the job of condensing an expository section of the narrative into a few hilarious minutes of action. What is most ingenious, though, is Richardson's use of cinematic counterparts to Fielding's literary methods. The film parodies old movies much as the novel parodies early literary forms. Another clever parallel is the celebrated dining scene between Tom and Mrs. Waters. Where Fielding extends for several pages a ludicrous metaphor of sexual battle, Richardson shows the couple devouring the meal while they devour each other with their eyes. The film replicates in moving images the novel's verbal tour de force.

There are other fine examples. Stuart McDougal (1985) has analyzed Jack Clayton's film, *The Innocents* (1961), to demonstrate how it duplicates in cinematic terms the verbal ambiguities of Henry James's novel, *The Turn of the Screw* (146–52). Where James uses a first-person narrator of questionable reliability, Clayton uses sound to underscore the subjectivity of our experience as viewers. Where James frames the governess's narrative with a testimony of her character, Clayton frames the body of the film with an interview. Thus Clayton balances the objective nature of photography against the film's codes of subjectivity in order to re-enact in cinematic terms the duplicities of James's point of view. *The Grapes of Wrath* (1940) presents another kind of challenge to the art of adaptation. John Steinbeck's novel is full of generalizations about politics and history which would be difficult to show on screen. McDougal shows how John Ford's film repeatedly converts abstractions to specifics by representing the displaced masses as a single family (1985, 31–35). Steinbeck's long discussion of corporate takeovers in Chapter 5 becomes a bulldozer that levels the Joads' home. An anonymous old woman sorting through her old possessions in Chapter 9 becomes a poignantly silent scene of Ma Joad and her hope chest on the eve of her departure. It almost isn't necessary when Ma says at the film's finale, "We'll go on forever, Pa. We're the people."

We should not forget, however, that many of the differences between literature and films are due not to artistic limitations of the media but to matters of business. As Bluestone puts it, "The Hollywood producer is governed less by the laws of aesthetics than by the laws of the marketplace" (1985, 38). Whereas a novel can make a profit with 20,000 copies, a movie must reach millions. And movies cost more to produce. Movies, then, must be mass-produced for a mass audience. This means that no film is wholly the product of a single author; it bears the signatures of many hands and countless social forces. It also means that filmmakers tend to be more responsive to a general audience and therefore to a more restricted range of tastes; they can't appeal to special interests in the audience if this means losing the main group.

The Influence on Other Media

The relationship between literature and film goes well beyond questions of adaptation. Literature has influenced the course of film and vice versa. Film directors like Robert Bresson, D. W. Griffith, and Ingmar

Bergman owe immense debts to their readings of the classics. Writers like John Dos Passos, Lawrence Durrell, and Thomas Pynchon have openly borrowed film techniques. Then there are those writers whose methods could be said to be, in some ways, cinematic; among them James Joyce, Charles Dickens, Gustave Flaubert, and Laurence Sterne. Here it is not a matter of influence, but of aesthetic affinity, artists working out ideas in one medium that would eventually find full expression in another.

Sergei Eisenstein, the Soviet film pioneer, credited Dickens with creating effects in his novels that parallel an extraordinary number of film techniques later used by directors like Griffith, including close-ups, dissolves, crosscutting, montage construction, and certain sound effects (1949, 195–255). Eisenstein took this as a sign of Dickens's keen visual sense and his ability to think in plastic forms. Further, he considered it good evidence that literature is, to a great extent, an art of seeing.

William Faulkner offers an even more intriguing case of correspondences between literature and film. Bruce Kawin has called Faulkner "the most cinematic of novelists" (1977, 5). Kawin has written the definitive study of Faulkner's work in Hollywood (*Faulkner and Film*) as well as editing the hitherto unpublished screenplays that Faulkner wrote for MGM (*Faulkner's MGM Screenplays*). Faulkner's experience with cinema ran the gamut. He collaborated on other people's films (*To Have and Have Not*, 1944; *The Southerner*, 1945; *The Big Sleep*, 1946) and he worked on adaptations of his own works, some of which made it to the screen (*Intruder in the Dust*, 1949), some of which did not (like *Barn Burning*). There are also film versions of his novels which he had no part in adapting, like *Sanctuary* (1961) and *The Reivers* (1969), and finally, there are those novels which Kawin considers cinematic in themselves, like *The Sound and the Fury*. To study the interplay between Faulkner's achievement as a novelist and his accomplishments in Hollywood is to explore the lively conversation between art forms that takes place within a great artist's work.

The exchange between literature and film has been explored more broadly by Keith Cohen. Cohen traces many of the innovations of the modern novel to cinema, arguing that "the contours of modern narrative would not be what they are without the precedents set by the movies" (1979, 10). While not insisting on direct influence, Cohen pursues a number of correspondences to arrive at some intriguing insights. For example, he compares the modern novelist's preoccupation with shifting points of view to the filmmaker's placement of a camera. The need in film to combine shots taken from different camera angles encourages a relativistic approach to storytelling. Cohen is suggesting that the mechanical requirements of cinema coincide with the thematic interests of writers like Joyce and Proust. Another coincidence is the way human and nonhuman figures appear on the screen. Motion pictures represent objects and people on the same level of existence, a phenomenon that is exploited for comic effect by Charlie Chaplin and Buster Keaton and, more seriously, by Franz Kafka and Samuel Beckett. Like other scholars, Cohen observes that cinema has also influenced literature by taking over some of its traditional roles. Just as photography displaced the representational function of painting, film nudged written fiction away from realism toward the task of depicting the inner life.

Film and the Other Arts

So far, we have been comparing film to narrative forms of literature, primarily the novel and short story. It's worth remembering, however, that silent movies were called "photoplays" and that many films today are still classified as dramas. In fact, much of the early cinema was modeled on the theater. The first "art films," in particular, depended on the stage for their subjects, performers, and techniques, yet most critics agree that film is most like film when it is free of the proscenium arch. Kawin contrasts the "unshifting presence" of the stage, where all motion is inscribed within a continuum of space and time, to the movie frame, which can transport us instantly to other times and places (1987, 394). Furthermore, the frame can redefine our point of view, bringing us closer to the action or letting us watch it from below. In contrast, the stage requires us to shift or focus our attention on our own. As Beja notes, "at a film more is done *to* and *for* us, and less *by* us, than at a play" (1979, 67). Then, because dramatic performances are live, we make different psychological connections to the action. Cohen expresses it this way: "While in the theatre the spectator is basically a witness, in the cinema he is more of a voyeur" (1979, 74).

Film has been compared to poetry, music, dance, and even architecture. This is especially true of non-narrative, experimental forms, which are less concerned with telling stories than with conveying moods and ideas. It's worth considering how a movie can be like, or unlike, a dance number or a musical composition. Some movies do include dances, poetry, or music, of course, but there is a difference between a filmed dance and a dance film. There is an even greater difference between the art of dance and the art of film. How do films handle the elements of rhythm or plastic form? How does a filmed experience compare to a live performance or the experience of walking through a cathedral?

Viewed from these perspectives, a movie adaptation is not so much an illustrated copy of a book but a new rendering of the story, to be appreciated on its own terms. The narrative terrain, with its significant settings, characters, and actions, is redrawn onto a different kind of map by a different sort of cartographer. For students of English, studying adaptations means learning about the possibilities and limitations of literary map making. By paying close attention to what is unique about each medium (What exactly do we get from a work of literature or film? What is added to or missing from the experience?), students become more aware of what it means to represent reality through fiction. By attending to the similarities between a movie and a book, they can come to recognize what is universal in all narratives, the motives and rewards of storytelling that transcend all media. If the movie makes them want to read the book, or vice versa, they may well conclude that one is better than the other. At least they will be in a better position to tell why.

2 The Languages of Film

It was Christian Metz who said, "A film is difficult to explain because it's so easy to understand" (Monaco 1977, 127). Metz, who spent a good deal of time trying to explain how movies work, was fascinated by their ostensible simplicity. Motion pictures seem so easy to produce (just point the camera and shoot) and to interpret (just sit back and watch) that we tend to think of them as natural phenomena. We forget that at the heart of film there is a language—actually several languages—that must be learned.

Making Sense of Movies

Consider how we come to understand what movies mean. How do we learn that when the image of an eye fills the screen, it means we're watching a close-up rather than a giant eyeball? How do we learn that when the screen gradually grows black, a scene has ended? When do we learn that when a row of houses glides across the screen, what is really moving is the camera, not the houses? Probably, we learned by watching lots of motion pictures. We grasped the significance of close-ups, fade-outs, and panorama shots while viewing them in otherwise familiar contexts, long before anyone taught us their names.

The fact that understanding movies is not automatic is illustrated many times in the early history of film. In the United States, during the days of silent movies, viewers were at first confused by flashbacks, crosscutting, and reaction shots, techniques understood by the youngest filmgoers today. When Robert Flaherty showed film clips of *Nanook of the North* to his Inuit friends in 1922, they failed to recognize themselves in the movie. Having had no previous experience with photography, they did not realize that the play of light and shadow on the screen was meant to represent their likenesses. Similar misunderstandings have been duplicated elsewhere in the world whenever film has not been seen before. In Russia, audiences thought that the close-ups in Eisenstein's *Potemkin* (1925) were photographs of severed limbs and heads. In Iran, a group of villagers being shown a health department film gasped in horror when they saw a close-up of some insects: "Thank Allah we don't have such large mosquitoes!" In a West African country, when each scene of a film ended in a fade-out, the spectators kept turning around to see what was wrong with the projector (Forsdale 1966, 612). These audiences had not yet learned the technical conventions of the cinema and its codes.

Although we often learn a language through exposure and practice just by living in the language environment, a more formal study of the language can make us more aware of how it works. English grammar offers a systematic way of understanding English. Similarly, we can appreciate the behavior of motion pictures systematically by studying the "grammar" of film. Film is not a language in exactly the same way that English is a language. There is nothing in a movie that corresponds precisely to a word, for instance, or a question mark, nor is the order of events in a movie as strictly regulated as the order of words in a grammatical sentence. For the moment, though, it will be helpful to look at film from a linguistic point of view.

Cinematic Grammar

The key to understanding any grammar is to understand the language as a system. Think of film as a system of images and sounds. The images may represent real objects, imaginary events, even ideas. The sounds may include music, sound effects, or speech. Filmmakers arrange these images and sounds systematically. The arrangement is meaningful to us because we understand the system. Let's take a short film sequence as an example. First, we see the image of a man standing on a bridge, a rope around his neck. Next, we see a close-up of his face. Beads of sweat form on his forehead. As he shuts his eyes, we hear the first strains of some banjo music. Then we see the image of a woman, elegantly dressed and smiling, seated on a garden swing and swaying gently to the music. Her motion is exceptionally slow. What does this sequence mean? How do we interpret it? We may guess that the man is about to be hanged. The rope and sweat are clues to his predicament. But what do the music and the woman have to do with him? Maybe there is someone on the bridge with a banjo. Maybe this woman is watching the event. More likely, though, the music and the woman represent his thoughts. We know that slow motion and special music in a movie often signal a flashback, a quick visit to the past. The fact that this slow-motion image follows a close-up of the man's face suggests that his mind is focused on the past. So we read the sequence as a subjective event: The man is thinking of his loved one at the moment of his death. What enables us to make sense of a film like this is our understanding of the systems of images and sounds, close-ups, and flashbacks through which filmmakers communicate meaning.

Photography can be regarded as a signifying system because photographs, like words, refer to things beyond themselves. A snapshot of a cat is not a cat, or else we couldn't slip it into our wallet. Yet photographs are more like the things they represent than words are. Photographs are likenesses; they bear a visual resemblance to some material original. Words usually are arbitrary sounds; the sounds represented by the letters *c-a-t* have no obvious similarity to the animal. That's why a non-native speaker is more likely to understand the picture than the word.

Signs and Referents: How Do Movies Signify?

Those who study signifying systems—semioticians or semiologists, as they are sometimes called—make a crucial distinction between a signifier and what it signifies. The sound and image of the word *cat* (its pronunciation and its spelling on the page) are *signifiers*. What speakers think of when using the word *cat* is the *signified*. The signified is not the animal itself, but a conception. Most likely, that conception involves mental images and personal associations formed through years of contact with furry, feline creatures. Semioticians use the term *sign* for the relationship between a signifier and the signified. A verbal sign is the relation between a sound-image and a concept. The actual animal—the thing to which the sign refers—its *referent*—is something else again. We'll leave that part to the zoologists.

What then is a photographic sign? Like a verbal sign, a photographic sign is a relation between the signifier and the signified. In this case, the signifier is the photographic image—patterns of shade and color on the screen—and the signified is the mental image—what those patterns evoke in our imagination. Because motion pictures are so lifelike, it's easy to forget that the signifier (what is projected on the screen) is not the signified (what we project in our imagination), or that the sign (a relation between the perceptual image and our conceptual response to it) is not the referent (what was in front of the lens when the camera was turned on). It's as if images of the world are transferred directly to the film stock, to the movie screen, and then to the inner screens of people in the audience, with very little effort or translation. This may help to explain why movies seem so real and why we rarely give much credit to the viewers for the mental work involved.

Yet it is important to remember that watching movies is an interpretative act. Despite the remarkable realism of photography, a photograph is still a sign, and signs must be read. Some images are more abstract than others. When Picasso represents a cat with a few circles and some squiggly lines, his drawing may be more challenging to read than, say, a painting by Mary Cassatt, especially by someone unfamiliar with the ways of abstract art. Similarly, Cassatt's painting or a Japanese woodblock print may be harder to read than a modern documentary film on cars. We can imagine a spectrum of signs ranging from the most abstract to the most specific. Words are more abstract than images, and drawings generally are more abstract than photographs. While the word *car* may represent any year or make of automobile, a pencil sketch begins to look more like a sports car or a sedan, and a photograph is more specific still.

The specificity of film creates special problems in interpretation. Writers can use words like *vehicle, automobile, station wagon,* or *Volvo* to indicate different levels of abstraction, but how do we know the intention of a filmmaker when what we see on the screen are 1985 Jaguars or 1990 Coupes de Ville? It seems that the language of speech is better equipped than the language of pictures for making direct statements. When I say, "This car is old," or "that car is fast," I'm making an assertion. But when I film a certain car, I'm not so sure how it will appear to viewers. I may manipulate the image to emphasize the car's age or speed, but essentially the image is a presentation rather than a statement. In this sense, visual and verbal texts require complementary forms of interpretation. Images evoke assertions; words evoke images. The audience completes the message by supplying mental words or pictures.

In addition to being more abstract and arbitrary, verbal language tends to be more analytic than film language. To describe a scene in English, we have to break down what we see into parts that can be represented word-by-word. An earthquake, for example, may take place in an instant, but the discrete nature of words forces speakers and writers to analyze the experience into linguistic bits: the rumble, a swaying chandelier, the sounds of falling bricks and shattered glass, the panic. Or take a simpler, more typical event: "The girl kicked the ball." The rules of English syntax compel us to distinguish among the action (kicked), an agent (the girl), and an object (the ball), even though it is difficult to picture the act of kicking without someone doing it or something being kicked. In this way, the language of film is more holistic. The photographic sign gives a less fragmented replication of experience. The whole quake can be pictured instantaneously. The kicker, the kicked, and the kickee can be represented as one event.

The fact that movies include sounds as well as photographs compounds the issue. The sound effects, background music, and dialogue of films may be studied as signifying systems in themselves. Sound effects, like photographs, resemble what they represent. The sound effect of horses' hooves bears an auditory likeness to the actual tramp of horses over cobblestone, although it may have been produced by coconut shells on a studio table. Music, on the other hand, tends to be more abstract. The swelling sound of violins may be more important for its evocation of emotion than for its reference to instruments; what the music usually signifies is pride or romance, not the presence of violins. Yet in some scenes, the musicians are clearly visible on screen, and what their music signifies may be primarily their role as musicians.

To understand such varieties of signification, it is helpful to borrow three terms from the American philosopher Charles Sanders Peirce. Peirce described three kinds of signs: icons, indexes, and symbols. An *icon* bears some similarity to what it represents. Photographs and sound effects are icons since they look or sound like their referents. An *index* bears a physical bond to what it represents. Smoke indicates fire; a sundial indicates the time of day. Yet there is no clear resemblance between smoke and fire or between a sundial and the passage of time: one signifies the other by virtue of a physical relationship. Fire produces smoke; the sun's movement over time produces a moving shadow on the sundial. A *symbol* is an arbitrary sign. It depends on an agreement among users to interpret it a certain way. Thus a flag becomes a symbol of a nation by common consent (Peirce 1955, 48–119).

Peter Wollen and other semiologists often emphasize that verbal language is primarily symbolic, while cinema is primarily iconic and indexical (1972, 143). For the most part, words are arbitrary. Their meanings are established by agreement among native speakers. The signs of cinema, by contrast, depend heavily on visual and acoustic similarity. The screen image of a cat or the pitch of its meow on a sound track are iconic because they resemble what they represent. These images and sounds are also indexical insofar as they depend on a physical connection to their referents. The photographic image was produced by light reflected from a real animal. The sound track was produced by recording actual noises.

Films bear the imprint of reality in ways that books do not. This is not to say that words are never icons. Onomatopoeic language—words like *buzz* and *rat-a-tat-tat*—works by virtue of auditory correspondences which may be recognized even by non-native speakers. Nor is cinema always indexical and iconic. When the clumping of hollow coconuts signifies the sound of horses or when violin music signifies romance, the relationship between sign and referent is neither simple nor direct. Motion pictures and their sound tracks often function symbolically. The villain's mustache, the iris shot, and the symphonic crescendo are symbols whose meanings are established by convention. We learn to interpret them by mastering the code.

Cinematic Codes: Syntagms and Paradigms

Semioticians study two orders of code, called syntagms and paradigms. They are often represented as two axes. The *syntagmatic axis* runs horizontally, unfolding in time. The order of words in an English sentence is governed by a syntagmatic code, the rules of syntax. "The cat bit the boy" has one meaning; "The boy bit the cat" has another. "Cat boy bit the" is virtually meaningless. The *paradigmatic axis* runs vertically. If you replaced the verb "bit" in the first sentence with another verb, say "kicked" or "kissed," you'd be exchanging elements from the same paradigm. Simply stated, syntagm refers to the order of words, and paradigm refers to the choice of words.

But what corresponds to words in a movie? What is a film's basic element of signification? John Harrington identifies the *frame* as a film's "smallest discernible unit" (1973, 8). If you examine a reel of film, you'll see that it's composed of many individual still photographs, called frames, printed end to end on a translucent celluloid strip. An average feature-length movie contains about 130,000 of these stills. During projection, the frames are flashed onto the screen one at a time, but so rapidly that the mind connects them into a seamless moving picture. The frame is more of a technological division than an artistic one, however, because filmmakers think not in terms of frames, but of shots. A *shot* consists of the frames produced by one continuous operation of the camera. Since any shot can be removed or rearranged during the editing stage of filmmaking, Harrington considers the shot to be the smallest functional unit of film, comparable to the word in spoken or written language (1973, 10). Shots, like words, can be taken out of context and recombined into new contexts to form new meanings, but as Harrington admits, shots differ from words in several respects. The high density of information in a single photograph can require hundreds of words to represent it verbally. In this sense, a shot is more like a sentence or a paragraph. It has its own internal structure.

Filmmakers have long understood, by training or instinct, that a framed space embodies certain principles of composition. Even the "empty" area of a blank screen has a kind of invisible terrain that we can explore by moving a shape within its borders. Rudolph Arnheim has shown how a disk within a square is subject to hidden lines of force. A single disk appears unstable when it is located slightly off center, but a second disk restores the balance when it is properly placed (1969, 11). An object in motion also seems to follow unseen forces. When it moves from left to right, it appears to be flowing with the current; when it moves from right to left, it encounters an intangible but noticeable resistance. Such psychological relationships between an object and its surrounding space, between figure and ground, have been studied carefully by scholars of film and other visual arts, who emphasize how much of viewing is interpretive (Wead and Lellis 1981, 70–73).

Visual and verbal signs differ in another way. The words of a spoken language already exist before the speaker chooses them. The English lexicon is finite. For the filmmaker, the visible world already exists, but each new image must, in a sense, be invented. No two shots, even of the same event, will be exactly alike. Because of changes in lighting, framing, movement, color, and the other variables involved in photographing an image, the filmmaker's lexicon, the paradigmatic range, is infinite. This open-endedness of photography, together with the fact that every image presents an indefinite amount of information to the viewer, is a major reason why film is not always regarded as a language. Yet, as film studies continue to point out, cinematic equivalents can be found for nearly every variety of speech, from metonymy to metaphor, from pun to cliché (Monaco 1977, 130–42; McDougal 1985, 242–86; Bluestone 1957, 20–31).

Questions about units of meaning, visual composition, and cinematic lexicons are essentially paradigmatic. They concern the choices available to filmmakers and viewers within a movie frame: the quality of lighting, camera angle, speed of action, acting style, or dress. The choices concerning how these frames are organized—the order of shots within a scene or scenes within a sequence—are syntagmatic. To study film syntax is to observe how shots are edited into a meaningful arrangement. Take a simple target-practice scene. It might begin with a long shot of someone with a raised rifle, followed by a medium shot of the target, then a close-up of a squinting eye, a close-up of a finger on the trigger, a close-up of the smoking barrel, a close-up of the target with a hole in it, and finally a medium shot of the person's smiling face. No surprises there. Most viewers would assume a bull's-eye.

Knowing what they know about the operation of firearms, the significance of smiles, and the order of events in films, they would connect
these individual shots into a coherent story. If the smile were replaced
by a scowl, or the target by another person (both paradigmatic changes),
it would be a different story. If the same shots were presented in a
different sequence (a syntagmatic change), it might also be a different
story. How would we interpret the scene if the close-up of the bullet
hole preceded the close-up of the smoking barrel?

Christian Metz has proposed one of the most ambitious schemes
for understanding film syntax. His *grande syntagmatique* identifies eight
distinct patterns by which cinema transforms the world into discourse.
In his words, the scheme "gives us a better outline of the *deep structure*
of the choices that confront the filmmaker for each one of the
'sequences' of [the] film" (1974, 123, emphasis in original). One pattern
is the *bracket syntagma,* a series of brief scenes representing a common
idea, as a familiar vignette of lovers running through a field, gathering
flowers, and riding a Ferris wheel might represent romance. Another
pattern is *parallel montage,* which cuts back and forth between two
simultaneous events, like the alternating shots of a heroine tied to the
railroad track, a galloping hero, and an approaching train in an old
silent movie. Metz recognizes that his "cinematographic grammar" is
not a real grammar in the usual sense, but simply "a body of partially
codified semantic implications." (1974, 223). Yet the scheme is useful
for comparing the structures of film narrative to spoken and written
forms of storytelling. Writers often use bracket syntagms to illustrate
abstract ideas and parallel montage to contrast and compare events.

One benefit of paying close attention to syntagms is the recognition
of how people organize the signs by which they represent reality into
meaningful compositions. Whether their stories are embedded in the
rules of written language or in the encoded sounds and images of
film, these compositions reflect the deeper structures of the mind. A
sustained comparison often begins by stressing similarities and ends
by emphasizing differences. The history of film semiotics has followed
such a course. Early theorists made bold claims for the analogy of
cinema and language partly to validate film as an art, bolstering its
status as an academic subject. Later on, as some of the more obvious
analogies wore thin and semiotics called for greater sophistication,
theorists became more interested in pointing out divergences between
cinema and other languages, underscoring their uniqueness. Even the
most ambitious semioticians, like Metz, have found the effort to be
scientifically precise and complete about the codes of film and its
correspondences to language something of a dead end.

What, then, are the lessons to be learned from this inquiry? First, as Robert Scholes has noted, semiotics reminds us that "much of what we take to be natural is in fact cultural" (1982, 127). Cinema and spoken discourse are based on systems that are learned. We can study codes of dress or manners as languages because we have forgotten that we have learned these things. The discipline of semiotics is, in Scholes's précis, "a continual process of defamiliarization; the exposing of conventions, the discovering of codes that have become so ingrained we do not notice them but believe ourselves to behold through their transparency the real itself" (127). Second, semiotics helps to shift attention from the author's intentions to the audience's expectations. It reminds us that meaning resides in both our manner of constructing messages and our manner of construing them within certain cognitive and cultural conventions. By recognizing that our students are interpreting the codes of cinema, we give them credit for what they know while engaging them in the process of investigating how they know. Finally, by looking for the structures—and the structuring abilities—which transcend a single medium, we move toward a broader understanding of thinking and communicating. This is not to say that we should reduce all filmmaking and writing to common terms, nor is the significance of any statement only a matter of paradigms and syntagms. When we think of meaning in cinema as a matter of experience—felt experience, shared experience, the life of the mind—we begin to connect film to everything that counts.

3 The Technology of Film

Film is an art, but it is also a technology. Whereas any writer can produce a novel with some paper and a pen, movies require cameras, film stock, sound equipment, editing machines, and more. Furthermore, technology demands technicians. A feature film may call for hundreds of specialists in lighting, cinematography, sound technology, makeup, costumes, set design, and special effects.

Students often want to know more about the machinery behind the movies and the individuals behind the machines. Where did King Kong's voice come from? Who trained all those birds in Hitchcock's thriller? How are wipes and fade-outs made? How do filmmakers combine the music, voices, and sound effects that add such realism and feeling to a film?

This section is for those who are curious about the technical side of motion pictures. It explains some basic principles on which movies are based. It describes some of the instruments behind the art of film. It traces the steps of film production, highlighting the people and the tools that make it happen. But this is not a story of technology alone. In the history of film, technology goes hand in hand with art. Technological advances bring fresh, creative possibilities; new artistic practices inspire scientific innovation. The cycle continues, like a revolving reel.

For readers whose curiosity extends beyond the scope of this chapter, there are some excellent resources. Bruce Kawin's textbook, *How Movies Work* (1987), has the best coverage I know of the technology of film. Instead of relying on other texts, Kawin has gone into the studios, labs, and archives of Hollywood to compile a current, accurate account of the whole production process, from conception to projection. Though technically precise, Kawin's analysis is lively reading, rich in instructive insights and entertaining illustrations of the art, business, and fun of film. Many of the examples and much of the information in this chapter are borrowed from Kawin's book.

One of the most popular treatments of film technology is Louis Giannetti's *Understanding Movies* (1988), now in its fifth edition. Giannetti includes chapters on photography, mise en scène (every element within a shot), movement, editing, sound, and acting. In James Monaco's *How To Read a Film* (1977), there is a useful chapter on "Technology: Image and Sound," as well as a handy glossary of film terms, although the book has not been reprinted since its original publication. A more thorough, though earlier, glossary is Harry Geduld and Ronald Gottesman's *An Illustrated Glossary of Film Terms* (1973). In 179 pages, this book defines the words most often used in the industry. For those who want a more recent introduction to the jobs behind the credits there is David Draigh's *Behind the Screen* (1988), printed by the American Museum of the Moving Image.

Tools of the Trade

Most people enjoy driving without knowing much about the engine, but knowing how a car works can increase both their mastery and appreciation of the vehicle. Knowing more about the instruments of cinema can bring similar benefits. It can often make the difference between simply viewing and truly seeing a film.

The Film. Photography is a chemical process. A photograph is formed when film coated with light-sensitive chemicals is exposed to light. The portions of this coating that receive the most light turn darkest, forming a negative image of the visual event. This *negative* makes it possible to reproduce the image, for when light is directed through the negative onto another piece of film, a *positive print* is the result. Sensitivity to light varies with film stock. A *fast film stock*, being more sensitive, is best for filming at night or whenever light is scarce. The problem is that fast film stock produces a grainier, less distinct image than *slow film stock*. Some filmmakers exploit this technical feature for artistic reasons. They use a faster stock to lend an unpolished, documentary look to a realistic scene.

Lenses. The camera's lens acts as a glass eye to focus rays of incoming light onto a strip of film. Lenses are classified by *focal length*, the distance from the plane of the film to the optical center of the lens when the lens is set to infinity. For a 35mm camera, a focal length of roughly 35 to 55mm produces something close to what we see with the human eye. This is the focal length of a normal lens, which gives the least distortion. A *wide-angle lens* (also called a *short-focus lens*), because it's shorter, takes in a wider field of view so that objects seem farther away. This also increases the illusion of depth and distorts linear perspective. A face filmed with a wide-angle lens looks rounder, with a longer nose and pinned-back ears. Camera operators have used this fact to exact revenge against the vanity of actors. By contrast, a *telephoto lens* (or *long-focus lens*), because it's longer, takes in a narrow field of view. The image looks closer. Since a telephoto lens compresses depth, objects moving toward or away from the camera appear to move more slowly. The famous shot of Dustin Hoffman running to the church in *The Graduate* (1967) was taken with a long lens to exaggerate the slowness of his progress. A long lens also has a shallower depth of field; there is a shorter range within which an image will appear in focus. This fact is useful when a filmmaker wants to isolate one face in a crowd or a lion in a field of grass. The features of normal, long, and wide-angle lenses are combined in the *zoom lens*, which allows the filmmaker to change the focal length during shooting. The camera can zoom in for a close-up or zoom out to a long shot while the action continues.

Shutter Speed. By itself, the lens would produce not a moving picture, but a blur. Something is needed between the lens and the film to stop the light just long enough so that the image frozen on a single frame of film can be moved out of position and a new frame moved in its place. This is done by a revolving plate called the *shutter.* The shutter in a movie camera usually revolves 24 times per second, the normal *shutter speed* for a sound film. With each revolution a new frame is photographed, so that twenty-four successive frames of film will be projected later as one second of motion picture film. We see motion, instead of individual frames, because the human eye is slower than the machine. The retina retains the image for an instant longer than the image is presented, just enough time for a new frame to replace it on the screen. This phenomenon, called *persistence of vision,* accounts for the illusion of smooth motion. In reality, we're watching a succession of still photographs. When film is shot at higher speeds, say 240 frames per second, the projected result is seen as *slow motion.* In this case, one second of filmed motion will be stretched out to ten. Slow motion is produced by *overcranking* the camera, a term left over from the days when film was cranked by hand. *Undercranking* produces fast motion. An action filmed at only 12 frames per second will be speeded up to twice its normal rate on the screen, a familiar trick in comic chase scenes.

The Screen. The audience's window on the world is defined by the four edges of the screen. The relationship between the horizontal and vertical dimensions of the screen is called its *aspect ratio.* A ratio of 1.33:1 (the *Academy ratio*) used to be standard, but times and standards change. In the early 1950s, *wide-screen ratios* were introduced, standardized in Europe as 1.66:1 and in the United States as 1.85:1. Since then, screens have been stretched into Panavision, CinemaScope, Todd-AO and other imaginative shapes, all of which require special screens or lenses to adjust the image. There are clear commercial motives behind these tinkerings with the image size, but there are artistic motives too. While the Academy ratio was long regarded as the best shape for most spatial compositions, it does not necessarily support the most interesting views. Think of what would be lost if the Super-Panavision of *2001: A Space Odyssey* (1968) were confined to standard proportions. Technology has also tried to add a third dimension to the screen. Three-dimensional (3-D) photography uses two lenses spaced 2½ inches apart to record a scene as if it were being viewed by a pair of human eyes. During 3-D projection, the two views are filtered by special glasses worn by all spectators, so that the image recorded by each lens is seen only by the corresponding eye. Kawin demonstrates how Hitchcock used this process effectively in *Dial M for Murder* (1954), but for the most part, 3-D movies have been little more than box-office gimmicks (1987, 167).

Shots and Angles. As noted earlier, a shot is a single length of film produced by a continuous running of the camera. Many filmmakers consider it the basic unit of film editing, although a great deal can happen in one shot. The elements within a shot—the action, dialogue, camera movements, choice of lenses, and so forth—are known collectively as *mise en scène*. Mise en scène refers to what happens on the set (literally, what is put into the scene), in contrast to the editing (*montage*) that happens after shooting.

Shots are conventionally defined by the size of the subject within the film frame. A *close-up* might show an actor's head or hand. A *medium shot* might show his body from the knees up. A *long shot* might show her entire figure running through a field. The definitions of these terms are not precise, and additional terms are often used for special cases, like *extreme close-up* or *medium long shot*. The subject's size may even vary within a single shot. For example, the camera may zoom in from a long shot of a mob to a close-up of the leader's face.

Most scenes are filmed from a normal height, at the subject's eye level. However, the *camera angle* may vary for particular effects. A *low-angle* shot is taken from below the subject. A *high-angle* shot is taken from above. Welles changes the angle of his camera in *Citizen Kane* to signal shifting points of view. Kane's campaign speech is seen from several perspectives. We see Kane loom larger than life from the low angle of an appreciative audience, then we see him from the extreme high angle of a balcony, where Kane's enemy is preparing to bring him to his knees. Elsewhere in the film, the camera angle gives a telling slant to individual shots. (See Figures 2 and 3).

Movement. The earliest cameras were fixed, but today the camera moves. It can *pan* a subject horizontally by pivoting left or right. It can *tilt* up or down by pivoting along a vertical axis. The camera can also move through space. When it moves horizontally—with, towards, or away from the subject—the result is called a *tracking shot.* Some cameras actually move on tracks; others move on wheeled platforms called dollies. For this reason, the horizontal camera movement is also called a *dolly shot.* When the camera moves vertically through space, sometimes lifted by a boom or crane, the result is called a *boom shot* or a *crane shot.*

Viewers sometimes confuse tracking shots with zooms. In a tracking shot, the camera moves. In a *zoom,* only the lens moves. A zoom lens is really a variable lens which can be moved toward the wide-angle position (for a long shot) or the telephoto position (for a close-up). Since the camera remains fixed in a zoom shot, the relative distances between objects remain constant, even though the objects may appear to grow or shrink in size. Contrast this with a tracking shot, which propels the viewer through space; objects near the frame's edge grow larger more quickly than objects near the center, creating a dynamic effect.

Lighting. Since movies are essentially recorded light, special attention is given to the technology of lighting. Cinematographers use several standard lighting styles, or "keys." The chief light illuminating the subject to be filmed is called the *key light.* In *high-key lighting,* the scene is flooded with bright illumination, giving it a cheerful, buoyant tone. In *low-key lighting,* illumination is low and soaked with shadows, creating an ominous or melancholy mood. Visitors to a movie set are often impressed by the number and variety of lights. *Spotlights* cast intense beams on the subject. *Floodlights* wash the scene with a less focused form of illumination. Sometimes a translucent shade, a *scrim,* is placed between the subject to soften the key light. *Fill light* provides a weaker, broader glow and is used to fill in shadows. An *eyelight* may be placed near the camera to add sparkle to the subject's eyes. A strong light from behind (*backlighting*) separates the subject from the background. Backlighting also creates a silhouette effect when the subject is not illuminated from the front. *Front lighting* generally softens a face, flattening the features and sometimes hiding facial marks.

Figure 2. A low-angle shot of Mr. and Mrs. Kane at breakfast.

Sidelight adds solidity and depth, accentuating features that give a face its character. Each lighting angle gives the filmmaker another tool for sculpting the subject.

Color. Although color films were not used widely until the late 1930s, filmmakers experimented with color from the start. Edwin Porter had individual frames painted by hand in *The Great Train Robbery* (1903). D. W. Griffith tinted certain scenes of *The Birth of a Nation* (1915) by dipping filmstock into colored dyes. He used blue tints for night scenes, red for the burning of Atlanta. Some of the best-known effects were used in *Gone With the Wind* (1939) and *The Wizard of Oz* (1939), both of which were filmed in *Technicolor,* a process in which the primary colors of an image are recorded on separate strips of film and recombined in the lab.

The Sound Track. There are four main kinds of sound in movies:

Figure 3. A high-angle shot of Kane and Leland outside the office of the *Inquirer.*

dialogue, sound effects, music, and voice-over. *Dialogue* and *sound effects* are usually synchronous; we see lips moving or cars colliding as we hear the words or clash of metal. *Music* and *voice-over* are usually not in sync with the picture. The music may come from an unseen orchestra; the voice-over may belong to someone not on screen.

All sounds are recorded on a *sound track.* In a single-system format, the most common, the sound track runs vertically alongside the picture on a strip of film. The sound track is usually magnetic or optical. A *magnetic sound track* is similar to audiotape. Sound is encoded on a stripe of magnetized particles which can be read by the magnetic head on a projector and converted back into sound. An *optical sound track* represents sound as a stripe of light bands, varying in density, which are read by a photoelectric cell in the projector and converted into sound. Unlike the images in a film, which stop and go through the projection system like individual slides, the sound track must pass the *sound head* of the projector in a continuous movement. That is why the sound corresponding to a given image is not alongside the matching frame. In 16mm film, the sound is 26 frames ahead of the picture.

Like images, sounds can be edited creatively. A sharp shift from one sound to another is called a *sound cut*. A gradual transition between sounds, the auditory equivalent of a dissolve, is called a *segue*. Sometimes the sound from one scene precedes the picture. Mike Nichols uses this technique quite often in *The Graduate* (1967). At one point, for example, Ben is in bed with Mrs. Robinson and we hear his father's voice, "What are you doing here?" The scene then shifts to Ben, who is lying on a raft in the backyard pool, squinting at his father's figure. The voice belongs to the pool scene, not the bedroom, but a significant connection has been made more strikingly through sound.

Special Effects. Increasingly more of the action in today's films is a matter of special effects. Nuns fly, giant marshmallows stalk the earth, live actors dance with cartoon rabbits. Not only are contemporary audiences amused by these improbable feats, they're fascinated by the technological wizardry behind them. Documentaries on the making of *Star Wars* (1977) or *Ghostbusters* (1984) are nearly as captivating as the feature films themselves.

At the heart of many special effects is the principle of *stop-motion photography*. In stop motion, shooting is interrupted at intervals while the scene is rearranged. *Animation* is created when a drawing or clay object is changed slightly every time the camera stops. When the film is projected at normal speed, the drawing or the object seems to move with a life of its own. *Pixillation* follows the same procedure, only with live people as the subject. An actor standing on one foot moves an inch forward. The camera shoots one frame. The actor inches forward in the same position again, and another frame is filmed. When the film is projected, the actor seems to glide across the screen on the same foot. Animation and pixillation can be tedious work. It takes about 14,400 frames to produce a ten-minute film (Monaco 1977, 106). Thanks to computers, though, the process is becoming easier to manage.

Ingenious special effects have been devised in the interests of time, money, safety, and imagination. When gorillas scale apartment buildings and moths devour Cleveland, the effect is usually achieved with *miniatures* or *model shots*. A small-scale model is filmed to look full size. The camera must be overcranked, (run at faster speeds) to slow down the action of the model so that it approximates normal motion. Today these small models can be big business. Steven Spielberg employed a colony of model makers and millions of dollars in equipment to supply the settings for his Indiana Jones and science fiction films.

When live actors interact with fictitious settings, the effect is often achieved with glass or matte shots. A *glass shot* uses scenery painted on transparent glass. The camera photographs the action through the glass so that the painted portions seem to be continuous with the action. The scenes of Xanadu in *Citizen Kane* were shot this way, with the hill and castle painted on glass. In a variation of this method called *rear projection*, the action is filmed in front of a screen while another action is projected on the screen from behind. This is how those shots of moving trains and taxis used to be filmed. The actors sat in a stationary vehicle while a movie of the landscape rolled past the "windows." A *matte shot* uses an opaque screen or matte to obscure certain portions of the frame. The film is exposed twice, first with one matte, then with a second matte that covers the area obscured by the first. When projected, the two separately filmed sections of the frame appear as a single image. This is how a cast of thousands stormed through medieval Paris in *The Hunchback of Notre Dame* (1939). First the action of the crowd was shot while a matte covered the outline of the city. Then the film was exposed again; this time a miniature model of old Paris appeared in place of the first matte while a second matte blocked out the crowd. The mattes were so carefully aligned that the combined images seem part of one continuous scene.

How Movies Are Made

Any major movie goes through four distinct stages: development, preproduction, production, and postproduction.

Development. A film starts with an idea. It may come from a book, an actual event, another film, or someone's raw imagination, but soon thereafter it goes through many transformations. Somebody may sketch out the main idea in a brief *synopsis* or *story outline*. Later this may be expanded into a *treatment*, a fuller version of the narrative which may contain scenes, character development, and some dialogue, much like a short story, but no detailed descriptions of the set or camera setups. Further along, a *scenario* or *screenplay* fleshes out the action, dialogue, and perhaps some directions for the camera. The most complete version before production is the *shooting script*, which usually gives a shot-by-shot blueprint of the film. Any of these versions of the story may be revised by other writers or studio personnel. Authorship is typically a collaborative enterprise.

In addition to script development, several key decisions are made before a film is given the green light. In large studios, specialists estimate expenses, investigate the market, and consider legal issues. Relatively few ideas make it past the development stage to preproduction.

Preproduction. Preproduction begins with the approval of a film project and ends just before the actual shooting. This stage includes a great deal of planning which few viewers ever think about. *Screen tests* are taken. The actors are cast. Locations are scouted. Background research is conducted. Sets are designed and decorated, props made, costumes fashioned and fitted. On a large production, these activities are carried out by a small army of specialists, including a casting director, production designer, art director, makeup artists, researchers, illustrators, draftsmen, set builders, propmakers, a set dresser, even a greens handler to take care of any flora used on the set. Eventually, the producer and assistants arrive at a final *shooting schedule* and *production budget.* Times and costs for filming each shot are worked out in detail. The film is ready for production.

Production. The main job of the *director* is to turn the screenplay into a film. Whereas the *producer* bears the ultimate responsibility for the final product, the director is responsible for directing the actors, supervising the technicians, and managing all action on the set. Some directors prefer to spend more time on preproduction than others. Most of Alfred Hitchcock's creativity went into scripting, casting, costumes, and art direction. For him, the task of shooting was mostly a matter of filling in the script. Other directors, like Federico Fellini, pay little attention to the script; their best ideas happen on the set. Still others, like Sergei Eisenstein, achieve their greatest effects after shooting, during the editing stage. On the whole, however, we think of directors as rulers of the movie set, perched on a canvas throne, giving the commands for "lights, camera, action."

Helping the director is a small crew of lieutenants. There may be one or more *assistant directors* to handle delegated tasks like planning the day's shooting, managing the extras, or keeping interlopers off the set. The *script supervisor* keeps track of the script, noting which shots are filmed, ever on the lookout for variant readings and visual discontinuities, like a change in lighting or the length of a lit cigarette (see Figure 4). A *cuer* and a *dialogue director* may help keep track of

Figure 4. From *Singin' in the Rain,* shooting a silent film. Left to right: the pianist creates the atmosphere, the script supervisor checks continuity, the director, the cameraman, and the assistant director look on.

dialogue and coach the actors with their lines. In a big production, there is simply too much for one director to coordinate.

Among the most important technicians on the set is the *cinematographer,* or director of photography, responsible for the camera work and related operations. While the director specifies the effect desired from each shot, this highly skilled individual usually selects the camera setup, lenses, film stock, and whatever else is needed to achieve that effect. In large crews, a *camera operator* will actually run the camera, while an assistant will *follow focus,* i.e., adjust the lens when the actors or the camera moves. Other crew members take care of lighting, sound, special effects, and so on. A *production mixer* decides how to set up the sound equipment for the best sound. Usually there are separate sound tracks for recording dialogue and live sound effects. The sound crew might also record *wild sound,* sound recorded separately from the picture, to be used as general background noise in the final film. If many shots must be taken of a single continuous action, like a dance, the action may be filmed to fit a prerecorded sound track, the *playback*. Later, the shots will be edited to match the music. Finally, no major set is complete without the gaffer, grips, and gofers. The *gaffer* is the chief electrician, responsible for lighting the set as directed by the cinematographer. The *grips* take care of equipment, sets, and props. The *gofers* run errands for everybody else, who order them to "go for this" and "go for that."

Apart from these technicians and assistants stand the *actors*, almost like a separate breed. Whether we think of them primarily as artists, celebrities, or human props depends partly on their status in the movie world, partly on their role within the film, partly on the director. Alfred Hitchcock was notorious for treating them like cattle, prodding them into roles fixed by the shooting script. Elia Kazan, on the other hand, gave his actors freedom to interpret character. Some of the best moments in Kazan's *On the Waterfront* (1954) were unplanned, impromptu lines and gestures that Marlon Brando discovered during the course of shooting.

A distinction is often made between two kinds of acting: method and technique. In *method acting*, performers try to get in character by identifying with the role. They may make an emotional connection between their characters' plight and events in their own lives, drawing on genuine feeling rather than relying on external acting techniques. The principles of method acting were developed by Soviet stage director Constantine Stanislavski and popularized in the United States by people like Elia Kazan and Lee Strasberg. Marlon Brando is a method actor. His strength as a performer lies in his ability to live his parts. *Technique acting* is more traditional. A technique actor like Bette Davis tries to convey character by imitating visible behavior. She might roll her eyes in rage, for example. Each gesture is a technique, a sign deliberately adopted to represent a given mood. Bruce Kawin neatly summarizes the difference between these acting styles in a brief story:

> When Dustin Hoffman (a method actor) got himself into his role for John Schlesinger's *Marathon Man* (1976) by staying up for days on end, breaking himself down so that he could fully realize the behavior of the tortured, bedraggled hero, Olivier [a technique actor] is said to have come up to him and asked, "But Dustin— wouldn't it be easier to *act*?" (Kawin 1987, 368).

On the set, the actor's life is not a very glamorous one. Instead of facing a live audience, he or she is usually eye to eye with an unblinking lens, speaking lines into a microphone instead of to another human being. The most intimate love scene must be played amid a crowd of technicians and machines. And since shooting schedules are arranged for technical convenience rather than dramatic continuity, actors learn to perform scenes out of order. This makes it difficult to steep oneself in a role or build a sense of character development. Screen actors must continually remind themselves who they are, what they want, and where they're going for each shot, and they must learn to do this on demand, repeatedly, since the director may request many *takes* (repeats) of the same shot.

A standard method for filming a scene begins with the *master shot,* a continuous long shot covering the entire action. Then portions of the action are filmed again, from different distances and angles. Later, the best shots will be selected and edited for continuity, using the master shot as a general guide. To assure continuity of action, the scene is *blocked,* usually by the director, by walking the actors through each movement before shooting. Critical points on the set are marked by tape or chalk so that the performers will always be in camera range. They quickly learn to *hit their marks* to avoid another take.

There is time for one more take. The actors are poised for action, sweating a little under the heavy lights. A makeup artist dabs the beads away. Wires and booms surround the set, just off camera. The gaffer adjusts a spotlight; the production mixer checks the needles on the sound equipment. Several grips stand by the dolly, ready to wheel the camera through the set. Standing near the director's chair, the script supervisor consults the script once more and nods. The director calls out, "Camera!" The camera operator turns on the camera and waits until the motor revs up to 24 frames per second before responding, "Speed." An assistant says, "Mark!" and snaps the clapsticks together smartly. Now the director calls, "Action!" Scene 5, Take 8 begins and continues until the director says "Cut!" The words everybody wants to hear are "Cut and print!" That means the take has been successful. Good takes (there may be several for any given scene) are printed overnight and viewed as *dailies* or *rushes* the next day by the director and the editor. The best takes are chosen, and if necessary scenes are reshot. The next step is postproduction.

Postproduction. With the set struck (dismantled) and the good takes in the can, the editor takes over. Usually with the guidance of the director, the editor assembles the raw footage into a continuous sequence, marking the places where optical effects (fades, dissolves, etc.) are to be inserted by the photographic lab, and assembling all the different sound tracks. Eventually the fine cut and all the tracks are sent to a sound lab, where music, dialogue, and sound effects are mixed to match the picture. The photographic lab then produces several generations of prints which result in the final release print that will be distributed to theaters nationwide.

Editing, or cutting, is the process of compiling a film from its constituent parts. The best shot is selected from the takes. Shots are arranged into scenes, scenes into sequences. A *scene* is usually composed of several shots of the same general action, time, and location, like the scene of Charlie's Colorado childhood in *Citizen Kane.* A *sequence* covers a broader range, but is unified by some thematic concern, like the marriage sequence in *Citizen Kane,* which is composed of five breakfast scenes spanning years of a relationship.

Technically, the process starts by cutting a roll of film into separate shots. Each shot may be labeled and hung over a *cutting bin* for easy access. Then the picture is matched with its corresponding sound, now recorded on *mag stock,* a length of magnetic sound tape. The editor *synchronizes* sound and image with the aid of a coupling machine like the upright *Moviola* or the flatbed *Steenbeck.* The usual trick is to locate the frame before each take in which the clapsticks meet and align it with the matching sound, a distinct bang on the mag stock. Once aligned, both picture (film) and sound (mag stock) are cut together. The editor's next task is to create a *rough cut,* usually by trimming the best shots and splicing them end to end into a tentative order. The *splices* are made temporarily with tape or, more permanently, with cement. The rough cut may be twice as long as the final film, in order to leave room for artistic experimentation. Later on, the editor creates a *fine cut,* a tighter version that will be screened for the executives. Once approved, a *final cut* is forwarded to the photographic laboratory for final processing.

The creative side of editing calls for a sense of rhythm, continuity, and the conventions of film narration. The editor might start a scene with an *establishing shot* to orient the viewer, like the shot of Manhattan's skyline which begins *King Kong.* In an action scene, he might add an *insert,* like the close-up of the villain's missing finger in *The 39 Steps* (1935). He might insert a *cutaway,* like the shot of a single crow which Melanie Daniels sees when she is sitting in the schoolyard in *The Birds* (1963). A dialogue might require several alternating *reverse-angle* shots, each speaker filmed from the other's point of view. Or it might call for a *reaction shot,* showing a character's reaction to some important action. When a single action is covered by two shots, most editors would make a *match cut* so that the second shot begins precisely when the first shot ends. Further, they would *match the action* by cutting at a visual turning point, like a boxer's jab to the chin or the moment of a torpedo's impact. Sometimes, though, editors create deliberate discontinuity with a *jump cut,* omitting part of the action between shots. Jean-Luc Godard uses this technique to jar the viewer into a higher level of awareness, much like Bertolt Brecht's alienation effect. Two simultaneous actions are often shown in alternating shots through the technique of *cross cutting,* or *parallel montage.* The old silent melodramas used this technique to alternate among the victim on the railroad tracks, the oncoming train, and the hero riding to the rescue. Cutting from one action to another heightened the suspense.

Some of the most striking visual effects are created in the lab. Transitions between shots, such as fades, dissolves, and wipes, are usually produced on an *optical printer,* a machine for filming film. The optical printer can re-photograph any frame and manipulate it visually. *Fade-outs* are created by darkening each successive frame. *Fade-ins* are created in a reverse manner. *Dissolves* are made by superimposing a fade-out over a fade-in, so that one shot seems to blend into the next. In a *wipe,* one image seems to wipe another off the screen. Images can also be reduced, enlarged (*blowups*), repeated (*freeze frames*), skipped (*fast motion*), or combined one over the other (*superimposition*).

Postproduction sound techniques, involving music, dialogue, and sound effects, have become highly sophisticated in recent years. It is not uncommon for a film to use a dozen separate sound tracks all blended into one. The *music track* (or tracks) may be created in a *scoring session,* during which the studio orchestra plays music specially composed or arranged for the scene. A musical *conductor* leads the orchestra while the film is being screened. The conductor may also have access to a *click track,* which measures each scene in frames per musical beat, or clicks. Click tracks are usually prepared by the *music editor,* whose main task is to coordinate the visuals with music written by the composer or arranger. The *dialogue track,* recorded during shooting, may actually be several tracks, one for each actor, so that the voices can be adjusted in relation to each other. Sometimes the voices are *dubbed* or *post-synchronized,* re-recorded in the studio. This is done when there was too much noise on the set, or when a movie filmed in one language is recorded into another, or when the script is altered after shooting. According to one account, Welles was forced to change one of the butler's lines in *Citizen Kane* after the film was shot. Raymond's appraisal of Kane, "He was a little gone in the head," was dubbed over in the studio: "He acted kind of funny sometimes" (Carringer 1985, 113). In addition to music and dialogue, most *sound effects* (abbreviated *SFX*) are added in the studio. These sounds may be selected from a library of standard sound effects or created on the spot. King Kong's voice, for example, was created by slowing down the recorded roar of a caged lion. The *sound-effects editor* may replace live sound effects with synchronized substitutes in a process called *Foley editing.* When all separate sound tracks are ready, they are blended in a process known as *mixing.* The tracks are combined into a single channel by means of a *mixing console.* The sound mixer controls the volume and quality of each track, adjusting an echo, making the music swell above the dialogue, letting the pounding waves segue or fade into a heartbeat. The resulting *composite master,* the final product of the mix, is sent to the photographic lab for synchronization with the negative print. Titles, credits, and optical effects will be added before producing the *release prints* for distribution and projection.

Film Production and the Classroom

What's the best way for students to learn about the process of producing films? One method is to make a film, or part of it. This is the most direct, most challenging, and most fun. Students work in production teams, taking charge of the film's script, shooting, sets, sound effects, or editing. As members of a team, they learn about group dynamics and individual responsibility, as well as film technology. Some guidelines for this option are given in Chapter 6 and Appendix 2.

Another method is to analyze part of a film very closely, taking note of the decisions that went into its production. Students select a scene and study its component shots, observing the action, camera work, lighting, effects, and sounds for each shot, as well as the transitions between shots. This option is described in Appendix 2 as the "Shot-by-Shot Analysis."

A third method is to research a particular phase of filmmaking, like acting or set design. Students choose some aspect of a favorite film—the choreography in *Singin' in the Rain,* Marlon Brando's role in *On the Waterfront*—find out more about it, and report on their findings. This option is described in Appendix 2 as "Behind the Scenes."

4 A Brief History of Film

The dream of capturing the flow of life and projecting it again as motion pictures is probably as old as dreams themselves. For centuries, people have known that if you make a pinhole in the wall of a darkened box, light from outside will shine through the hole and cast a moving image on the opposite wall. As early as the Renaissance, Italians called such a box a *camera obscura*, or dark room, and wondered how to fix the image to the wall. It was not until the nineteenth century that inventors discovered how to make lasting copies of the image. In the 1820s, an Englishman named William Talbot experimented with images on paper negatives, trying to "write with light" through the marvel of photography. By 1839, the French chemist Louis Daguerre had perfected a process for reproducing sharp, permanent images on treated metal plates, called Daguerrotypes. Meanwhile, various inventors had been tinkering with a phenomenon known as "persistence of vision." This is what happens when the retina retains an image of any object for a fraction of a second in the dark. Because our view of the object persists, a succession of still images can appear to move as one if they are properly presented to the eye. The inventors gave their ingenious toys sophisticated Greek names—the Thaumatotrope, the Zoetrope, the Phenakistascope—but they were little more than curiosities. It was not until the principles of the camera obscura, persistence of vision, and the Daguerrotype were combined that motion pictures as we know them were born.

Exactly when this happened is a matter of debate among film historians. Some give credit to Louis Le Prince, a Frenchman who produced several strips of film in Britain as early as 1888. Little is known of Le Prince, however, because he and his equipment vanished in 1890, after boarding a train for Paris. Other scholars cite the work of Thomas Edison's assistant, William K. L. Dickson, who used a roll of celluloid film (a medium perfected by George Eastman) to record sequential photographs in his Kinetograph of 1891. Perforations in the film allowed it to be lifted into place behind a shutter and exposed to flashes of light, frame by frame. Later, when the pictures on these frames were viewed through Dickson's Kinetoscope, a peep-show device, persistence of vision created the illusion of a fluid motion. But a peep show is not a movie screen, and so some historians credit the first real motion picture to two Frenchmen, August and Louis Lumière, who used their own invention, the Cinématographe, to record and project motion pictures for a theater audience in 1895.

Soon the Lumière brothers had another rival, a French magician named Georges Méliès. Whereas the Lumières were serious inventors interested in capturing reality on film, Méliès was fascinated by the new medium's capacity for trickery and spectacle. According to his own account, he was filming the traffic in Paris when the mechanism jammed. Méliès got it to run again, but when the film was later projected, he made a curious discovery: A taxi that had been passing when the camera stopped seemed to turn into a hearse. With further experimenting, Méliès learned to use stop-motion photography to make actors disappear, and soon his bag of special effects included fades, dissolves, and superimposition. So while the Lumière brothers filmed trains entering a station or workers leaving a factory, Méliès was making movies like *A Trip to the Moon* (1902) and *The Palace of the Arabian Nights* (1905). As early as the turn of the century, cinema had already taken the forked paths of reality and fantasy.

It is difficult to say precisely who invented each new film technique. Perhaps it doesn't matter very much. What seems most important is that the earliest practitioners extended the language of film, deliberately or through trial and error, while trying to tell their stories. Edwin S. Porter learned how to build sequences from individual shots while recounting *The Life of an American Fireman* (1903). For *The Great Train Robbery* (1903), he cut between indoor and outdoor scenes without playing each scene to its dramatic conclusion. While that would be unthinkable in a stage play, it seemed a logical way to shoot a film. Another American movie pioneer, D. W. Griffith, discovered innovative uses for close-ups, long shots, traveling shots, pans, and crosscutting in the course of his remarkable career, from one-reel melodramas like *The Adventures of Dollie* (1908) to large-scale epics like *Intolerance* (1916). Film by film, the medium of motion pictures was growing away from its dependence on staged action to become an independent art form.

The Rise of a New Art Form

To be sure, most run-of-the-mill film productions leaned heavily on theatrical models and inexpensive formulas. They were still considered

cheap entertainment for the masses well into the years of World War
I. Then, as new studios began turning out full-length features, movies
became more widely acceptable, middle-class fare. The Hollywood
moguls got their start during this period, among them Carl Laemmle,
Adolph Zukor, Jesse Lasky, Samuel Goldwyn, Louis B. Mayer, and
Jack Warner. Their shrewd business deals formed the large studios—
like Universal, Paramount, MGM, and Warner Brothers—which in turn
ruled the American movie industry for the next three decades.

In the early silent features we already find many of the roles and
genres that characterize so much of American cinema. Theda Bara
(her name was said to be an anagram for "Arab Death") played the
exotic vamp, while "Little Mary" Pickford played the Virgin in Per-
petual Peril. William S. Hart became the rugged Western hero who
prefers his horse before his girl, while Douglas Fairbanks became the
prototype for all urban, urbane idols. Meanwhile, D. W. Griffith's artful
melodramas and Mack Sennett's wacky comedies laid the cornerstones
for screen tragedy and comedy on which other directors (Cecil B.
DeMille, King Vidor, Henry King, Erich Von Stroheim, Ernst Lubitsh,
Charlie Chaplin) and actors (Clara Bow, Pola Negri, Gloria Swanson,
Greta Garbo, John Barrymore, Ronald Colman, Lon Chaney, Harold
Lloyd, Harry Langdon, Buster Keaton) were soon to build.

The 1920s witnessed other trends in other countries. In Germany,
a strong current of expressionism produced haunting films like *The
Cabinet of Dr. Caligari* (1920), *Nosferatu* (1922), and *Metropolis* (1926).
Unlike the entertaining dreams of Hollywood, these German films
explored subjective images of horror interlaced with psychological and
social themes. Robert Wiene's *Caligari* is a stylized portrait of insanity;
Fritz Lang's *Metropolis* is an allegorical study of the class system and
its monumental inhumanity. It is hard to imagine such pictures, with
their focus on ideas rather than on performance, emanating from the
studios of Paramount or MGM.

In the Soviet Union, directors were anxious to capture the spirit of
their new revolution on film. Lacking the film stock for producing
movies, they concentrated first on editing techniques. Lev Kuleshov,
Dziga Vertov, Vsevolod Pudovkin, then Sergei Eisenstein learned the
power of manipulating images. Working with Hegelian notions of
thesis and antithesis, Eisenstein fashioned an elaborate theory of
montage to show how individual shots of film can be joined in a
creative synthesis of ideas and ideology. While Eisenstein owes much
to his studies of Griffith, the movies he produced during these times,
like *Strike* (1925) and *Potemkin* (1925), deliberately replaced the Hollywood story line with a documentary-style chronicle of events and

substituted a new kind of mass hero for the individual star. So German and Soviet cinemas, each in its own way, moved away from Hollywood's example along different national paths.

By the 1930s, the motion picture industry was at its peak. In 1938, for instance, 80 million Americans were going to the movies every week. That was 65 percent of the population. More than 500 features were produced by Hollywood the previous year. Compare those figures to 1968, when only 20 million (10 percent) attended movies weekly, or to 1969, when no more than 175 features were made (Mast 1981, 225). There were several reasons for this surge. The introduction of sound in the late 1920s and its artistic exploitation in the 1930s enlarged the range of motion pictures and broadened their appeal. The Depression put millions out of work and created a huge market for inexpensive entertainment offering escape from the troubles of the day. Hollywood's studios were willing to provide this entertainment in abundance, using mass production methods that would be the envy of Henry Ford.

The genres of the 1930s typically reflected the times or deflected attention toward some glittering dream. A succession of gangster movies (*Little Caesar*, 1930; *Public Enemy*, 1931; *Scarface*, 1932) captured the grittiness of big city life, as did tough-talking stories about news reporters (*The Front Page*, 1931; *Front Page Woman*, 1935). At the other extreme, a wave of musicals (*Flying Down to Rio*, 1933; *Top Hat*, 1935; *Gold Diggers of 1933*, also *1935*, and *1937*) and screwball comedies (*It Happened One Night*, 1934; *Bringing Up Baby*, 1938) stressed the bright side of things. Theda Bara and Mary Pickford were replaced by Mae West, Marlene Dietrich, Carole Lombard, and Claudette Colbert. William S. Hart and Douglas Fairbanks were succeeded by a galaxy of stars, including Clark Gable, James Stewart, Errol Flynn and Charles Boyer. Some actors, like Jimmy Cagney and Paul Muni, created a new type of Depression hero whose toughness and unabashed ethnicity appealed to those for whom the American Dream had recently turned sour.

As the major studios gained power, they became associated with certain kinds of films. Paramount specialized in witty, sophisticated, "European" dramas; MGM appealed to the American middle class; Warner Brothers produced movies with the feel of social documentaries; RKO made sophisticated musicals and comedies; and Universal specialized in low-budget genres, especially Westerns and horror films. It was a little like the assembly plants of Detroit specializing in Cadillacs or Buicks, with each studio hiring directors to carry out its own production goals. Paramount's Josef Von Sternberg, MGM's Victor

Fleming, Warner's Michael Curtiz, and Universal's Tod Browning all bore the stamps of studio policy as often as they put their individual imprints on the films they made.

The 1930s were particularly good years for French cinema. While Germany mobilized for war with films like *Triumph of the Will* (1935), and Russia prepared for its defense with films like *Alexander Nevsky* (1938), France enjoyed a golden age of screen diversity. René Clair entered the sound era with two popular musicals and a cautionary tale about industrialization (*A Nous la Liberté*, 1931) that prefigures Charlie Chaplin's *Modern Times* (1936). Jean Cocteau continued his avant-garde experiments, Jean Vigo produced two masterpieces of poetic realism (*Zéro de Conduite*, 1933; *L'Atalante*, 1934), a tradition carried on by Jacques Feyder and Marcel Carné. But the most influential director of this period was Jean Renoir, who created such enduring works as *Grand Illusion* (1937) and *The Rules of the Game* (1939).

Cynicism and Post-War Decline

For the United States, the Depression ended with the entry into World War II. With it, the genres of the 1930s took on a darker cast. The formula for screwball comedy acquired a strong dose of cynicism (*His Girl Friday*, 1940; *Meet John Doe*, 1941) and reflexivity (*Sullivan's Travels*, 1941). The romance of the thirties' gangster movies shaded into the hard-boiled pessimism of film noir (*The Maltese Falcon*, 1941; *The Big Sleep*, 1946). Some directors of the thirties, like Frank Capra, John Ford, and Howard Hawks, adopted a more skeptical tone. New directors, like Orson Welles, arrived with their skepticism full-blown. Welles's masterpiece *Citizen Kane* (1941) is probably on more ten-best lists than any other movie. Although it owes much to German expressionist imagery and French poetic realism, its self-conscious innovations in photography and editing made it a landmark in American cinema and a highly influential film for years to come. It is probably the most thoroughly studied movie ever made.

The war left European moviemaking in a shambles. Facilities in Germany, France, and Russia were virtually destroyed. In Italy, however, where an early surrender left the industry more or less intact, filmmakers were able to begin the movement which became widely known as neorealism. It began with Luchino Visconti's *Ossessione* (1942) and reached the world with Roberto Rossellini's *Open City* (1945), films which take the camera out of the studio and into the streets. Vittorio De Sica's *Bicycle Thief* (1948), probably the most popular neorealist film today, illustrates the emotional power that can be achieved by shooting an unformulaic story with nonactors and without sets on grainy film stock—the complete antithesis of Hollywood studio productions.

The taste for serious, realistic movies was probably only a small factor in Hollywood's postwar decline. True, the "social consciousness film" enjoyed a vogue with American audiences. Elia Kazan turned to serious subjects like anti-Semitism in *Gentleman's Agreement* (1947) and racism in *Pinky* (1949). In 1949, directors were tackling themes like Southern demagoguery (Robert Rossen's *All the King's Men*), juvenile delinquency (Nicholas Ray's *Knock on Any Door*), and corruption in sports (Robert Wise's *The Set-Up*). But some old genres, notably musicals (*Singin' in the Rain*, 1952; *South Pacific*, 1958) and comedy (*Scared Stiff*, 1953; *The Seven Year Itch*, 1955) survived into the 1950s. And others, like science fiction and the Western, emerged as the most popular film forms of the next two decades. While outer space and the frontier were hardly new to motion pictures, they became central concerns in movies like Robert Wise's *The Day the Earth Stood Still* (1951), Fred M. Wilcox's *Forbidden Planet* (1956), Fred Zinnemann's *High Noon* (1952), and John Ford's *The Searchers* (1956).

Meanwhile, the giant studios were breaking up. Financial problems, political threats, and the arrival of television were beginning to take their toll. Hollywood fought back with a round of gimmicks and inventions. In an effort to regain its audiences, it sought to entice them with highly publicized campaigns for Technicolor, Cinerama, CinemaScope, 3-D, and blockbuster films (*Ben Hur,* 1959; *Spartacus,* 1960; *Exodus,* 1960), but the studio system's power weakened year by year. It was time for independent producers to take over.

Independent Voices and Distinctive Styles

The American audience was changing with the times. By the mid-1960s, it had become a younger, better-educated, more affluent group. It had also become smaller. While older viewers generally stayed home with the family television set, the younger audience went out to see a new, sophisticated brand of film, typified by *Bonnie and Clyde* (Arthur Penn, 1967), *2001: A Space Odyssey* (Stanley Kubrick, 1968), and *The Wild Bunch* (Sam Peckinpah, 1969). Films like Haskell Wexler's *Medium Cool* and Dennis Hopper's *Easy Rider* (both made in 1969) introduced a new level of violence and social protest, reflecting the counterculture that developed in response to Vietnam.

In the 1970s, as the country moved from the upheavals of an unpopular war to the economic uncertainties of inflation, the industry experimented with a series of disaster films (*Airport,* 1970, 1974, 1977), gangster films (*The Godfather,* 1972, 1974), horror films (*The Exorcist,* 1973, 1977), and space films (*Star Wars,* 1977) among others. Meanwhile, individuals like Woody Allen and Robert Altman were producing films like clockwork. Allen directed ten films in as many years; Altman directed fifteen. Many of the new directors, unlike their learn-on-the-job predecessors, were graduates of film schools: Francis Ford Coppola and Paul Schrader (UCLA), George Lucas and John Milius (USC), Martin Scorsese and Brian De Palma (NYU). Not surprisingly, their productions sometimes showed the mark of academic study, but more often they succeeded in creating vigorously original images and stories for yet another generation. By the mid-1970s, critics were talking about a Hollywood Renaissance.

New Currents in the Stream

Meanwhile, African Americans, women, and other groups that have been underrepresented or misrepresented in mainstream cinema are starting to emerge, not only in more balanced images on the screen, but also as directors, script writers, editors, and other shapers of those images.

Scholars are now rewriting the history of black cinema to keep up with these changes. Thomas Cripps has meticulously traced the role of black performers from the demeaning racial stereotypes of silent films to the liberal studio codes of 1942 (*Slow Fade to Black,* 1977). Gary Null has extended the record through the urban black adventure movies of the early 1970s (*Black Hollywood,* 1975). Donald Bogle's account continues the story to include the bright young directors of the 1980s (*Toms, Coons, Mulattoes, Mammies, & Bucks,* 1989).

Most roles available to black performers before World War II were limited to comic or menial bit parts. Bogle classifies them in five categories, noting that all five types appeared in Griffith's epic story of the Ku Klux Klan, *The Birth of a Nation* (1915), a film that was all the more harmful because it was well made. Many of these roles were played by whites in blackface, a practice that continued well into the 1930s and beyond. At the same time, a small number of independent "colored" companies attempted realistic portrayals of black Americans in films like *The Birth of a Race* (1919) and *Dark Manhattan* (1937) (see Cripps 1977, 70–89, 170–202; Bogle 1989, 101–116). While they could not compete with the big-budget gloss of Hollywood, these companies produced a steady stream of movies for the four hundred or so black theaters they served until the 1940s. Chief among the independents was Oscar Micheaux, a novelist turned entrepreneur who wrote, directed, and produced thirty-four movies in thirty years. Operating on a shoe-string budget and Hollywood-like hype, Micheaux would feature his performers as the "black Valentino" or the "sepia Mae West," using advances from theater managers to finance his next film.

With the coming of sound, Hollywood invented the "all-singing, all-dancing, all-black musical," notably *Hallelujah* (1929) and *The Green Pastures* (1935). These musicals continued to provide occasional employment for African Americans well into the 1950s with films like *Cabin in the Sky* (1943), *Carmen Jones* (1954), and *Porgy and Bess* (1959), but the best-paid performers of the era were character actors, like high-steppin' Stepin Fetchit, Bill ("Mr. Bojangles") Robinson, and Hattie McDaniel. In 1936 alone, McDaniel appeared in eleven films, invariably as a servant. Explaining her Oscar-winning role as Mammy in *Gone With the Wind* (1939), she once said, "it's much better to play a maid than be one" (Null 1975, 76). The most impressive talent to break the typecast barrier was Paul Robeson, who played the title role in *The Emperor Jones* (1933) with a white supporting cast. Robeson was an extraordinary intellect, athlete, and performer, but he left Hollywood disillusioned in 1936 and spent the remainder of the decade in Great Britain. In the 1950s, Sidney Poitier became the nation's best-known and most versatile black actor, taking serious roles as a priest (*Cry, the Beloved Country*, 1951), an urban high school student (*Blackboard Jungle*, 1955), a convict (*The Defiant Ones*, 1958), and a soldier (*All the Young Men*, 1960).

Hollywood often trails closely behind cultural realities. The sensitive, socially relevant movies of the 1960s (*A Raisin in the Sun*, 1961) were followed by the so-called "blaxploitation" movies of the 1970s. Typically patterned on escapist fantasy, these commercial films replaced Humphrey Bogart and James Bond with black figures like Richard Roundtree (*Shaft*, 1971) and Ron O'Neal (*Superfly*, 1972). But they were made by black directors—among them Ossie Davis, Melvin Van Peebles, Gordon Parks, Sr. and Jr.—and arguably led to the creation of a new urban black aesthetic. The seventies and eighties also introduced new acting talent (James Earl Jones, Cecily Tyson, Richard Pryor, Whoopi Goldberg) and some serious new themes (*The Great White Hope*, 1970; *Sounder*, 1971; *An Officer and a Gentleman*, 1982; *A Soldier's Story*, 1984). Prospects for the 1990s look more promising than ever, especially for young black directors. In the wake of successes by Spike Lee (*Do the Right Thing*, 1989), Euzhan Palcy (*A Dry White*

Season, 1989), Mario Van Peebles (*New Jack City,* 1991), and John Singleton (*Boyz N the Hood,* 1991), the studios have been searching the film schools for gifted African American filmmakers. More black films were scheduled for release in 1991 than in the entire previous decade (Bates 1991, 15).

As with African American cinema, new histories are being written from feminist, Third-World, and other perspectives considered marginal in traditional histories of film. I have suggested further films and readings which illustrate some of these perspectives in the sections on *Do the Right Thing* (1989), *Sugar Cane Alley* (1984), and *Awakenings* (1990).

New Waves Abroad

Since the 1950s, wave after wave of filmmaking activity has swelled, crested, and spread its influence around the world. The first new wave began in France. After World War II, filmmakers like Robert Bresson, Jacques Tati, and Max Ophüls had originated highly personal directorial styles. Critics used the term *auteur* to emphasize that such directors were the authors of their films, more like the authors of books than most earlier directors hired to oversee the collaborative efforts of large studios. Some of the critics who proposed this auteur theory tried their own hand at directing, contributing to a "new wave" (*nouvelle vague*) in French cinema. While their films were individual creations, they shared certain characteristics—the use of hand-held cameras, natural lighting, shooting on location, improvised plots, and deliberately disruptive editing techniques—which gave them the look of *cinéma vérité*, movies that seemed more true to life because they lacked the polish of professional films. The new wave reached a peak in 1959 with Alain Resnais' *Hiroshima, Mon Amour* and François Truffaut's *The Four Hundred Blows,* then gained steady momentum as fresh talent like Louis Malle, Eric Rohmer, and Agnès Varda contributed their creative energies.

The French new wave was highly influential abroad, particularly in Britain, where the English studios, built up in the 1930s by Alexander Korda and Michael Balcon, had been languishing. The new impulse from the continent helped to stimulate a British "New Cinema," advanced in the 1950s by the work of Karel Reisz, Tony Richardson, and Lindsay Anderson, and continued throughout the 1960s and 1970s by John Schlesinger, Bryan Forbes, Joseph Losey, Richard Lester, and Ken Russell. The British cinema has produced a steady stream of high-quality movies ever since.

In Italy, those who learned their craft from the neorealists developed distinctive styles during the 1960s and 1970s. Federico Fellini and Michaelangelo Antonioni won worldwide recognition for their films, as did, to a lesser extent, Pier Paolo Pasolini, Ermanno Olmi, Bernardo Bertolucci, and Lina Wertmuller.

In Germany, a movement called *das neue Kino* (the new cinema) grew out of a meeting of ambitious young filmmakers in Oberhausen. Their manifesto, published in 1962, became the impetus for a radical shift in German cinema, from postwar "rubble films" to the bold, sensuous, richly ambiguous films of Volker Schlöndorff, Rainer Werner Fassbinder, Werner Herzog, and Wim Wenders.

Meanwhile, on the other side of the globe, Japan gradually emerged from its cinematic isolation of the prewar years. The first to break through to international audiences was Akira Kurosawa, with *Rashomon* (1950), an intriguing tale of rape and murder told from multiple points of view. Kurosawa's films bore clear marks of Western influence, but they cleared the way between Western filmgoers and more traditional Japanese directors, like Kenji Mizoguchi and Yasujiro Ozu in the 1950s and Masashiro Shinoda and Nagisa Oshima in the 1960s.

Renaissance in Eastern Europe

The 1960s witnessed an extraordinary burst of filmmaking activity in another corner of the world, in Eastern Europe. Among the countries most dominated by Soviet policies since Stalin, film had long been recognized as an important social and political force. In Poland, Hungary, Czechoslovakia, and Hungary—all nations of the Soviet bloc—the motion picture industries revolved around state-governed film schools that controlled the means of production, the professional training, and the kinds of films being made. From the 1940s to the 1960s, these schools concentrated chiefly on local political and economic issues, their films being heralds of the state. Then, as policies became more liberal, they began producing movies that appealed to larger audiences. In Poland, directors like Andrzej Wajda, Jerzy Skolimowski, and Roman Polanski became international figures. In Czechoslovakia, there were Jiří Trnka, Ján Kadár, Jiří Menzel, and Miloš Forman. There was Miklós Jancsó in Hungary, Dušan Makavejev in Yugoslavia, and Georgi Stoyanov in Bulgaria. When Soviet pressure put a stop to the Eastern European Renaissance, some of these directors fled to the West. Polanski and Forman, for example, have been making movies in English.

It will be interesting to see if the end of the Cold War brings another

Renaissance during the 1990s. Even in the Soviet Union itself, as Stalinist restraints have withered away and the Iron Curtain collapsed, more and more movies have made their way to theaters in the West. International film viewers have become familiar with names like Andrei Tarkovsky, Pyotr Todorovsky, and Nikita Mikhalkov, who represent a new generation of Soviet directors.

A New Internationalism

Not every nation has experienced a new wave. Some countries are represented in the world's eyes mainly by a single, often singular directing talent. Sweden has its Ingmar Bergman, India its Satyajit Ray. This does not mean that Sweden or India has not produced other good filmmakers, nor does it mean that other countries have not produced good films. The Third World, for example, has been especially active in recent years. In Africa, Ousmane Sembene has achieved international status for his films about life in Senegal. In South America, the Brazilian director Gláuber Rocha led a movement, called *cinema novo,* which spread throughout the continent during the 1960s. *The Hour of the Furnaces,* by the Argentine directors Fernando Solanas and Octavio Getino (1968), *Lucia,* by Cuba's Humberto Solás (1968), and *The Blood of the Condor* (1969), by Bolivia's Jorge Sanjines and the *Grupo Ukamau,* were among the first of many in this militant new wave of Portuguese- and Spanish-speaking films.

As cinema approaches its hundredth year, some filmmakers have begun to cut across national boundaries toward a new internationalism. Movies like Roland Joffe's *The Mission* (1986), Nikita Mikhalkov's *Dark Eyes* (1987), and Wim Wenders's *Wings of Desire* (1988) are made in several countries, in several languages, with casts and crews of several nationalities. The reasons for this international collaboration are political and economic, as well as aesthetic: Filmmakers can avoid local restrictions, draw on a wider range of resources, and reach a wider audience.

It may still be too soon to appraise the 1980s or speculate about the 1990s. After years of general decline, the industry seems to be flourishing again throughout the world, aided by advances in technology and the favorable market trends of multiplex cinemas, cable television, and videocassettes. But technical and monetary progress do not guarantee artistic achievement. We've come a long way from the dark ages of the camera obscura. Whether we will realize the full, bright potential of the *camera lucida* remains to be seen.

In this chapter, I have left out a great deal. I haven't mentioned Alfred Hitchcock, Howard Hawks, or George Cukor, for example. Nor have I said much about Australian, Chinese, or Canadian film. This is not so much a matter of oversight as of spatial constraint. To be brief, I have had to exclude a number of important names, countries, and entire histories of film. A more complete view would include documentaries and independent films. It would include the names of cinematographers, performers, and set designers, as well as individual directors. A technological history would trace the development of inventions, as well as artists, examining the impact of cameras, color, sound, and screens on the state of the art. An economic history would regard film as an industry, with chapters on the studio system in the United States, state control within the USSR, methods of production, distribution, and exhibition. A social history would stress the changing audience, reflecting changes in the times. Many of these histories are available in other books, and I have listed some of these as references. Still other histories of film are waiting to be written.

5 Theories of Film

Sooner or later, most teachers begin to look at any subject they are teaching as a whole. If you've been introducing films into your classes now and then, it's natural to make connections between films, to link your individual insights into a coherent pattern that is larger than any single film. What may have started as an occasional diversion becomes, with further thought and systematic study, a deeper understanding of the principles which underlie the magic of the movies. It is this search for underlying principles that leads us to theories of film.

Like theories of literature or composition, theories of film attempt to answer fundamental questions of identity, process, and effect. How is cinema different from the other arts? How does it work? What are the sources of its aesthetic, social, psychological, and ideological power? As in other fields of study, certain film theories have had their camps, their champions, their moments of ascendancy and decline. The realists have stressed the recording properties of film, its special ability to capture slabs of life on celluloid. The formalists have focused on film's expressive and manipulative powers, emphasizing the medium's capacity to transform the visible world into private or collaborative visions of reality. Advocates of the auteur theory have seen movies primarily as works of individual artists; they view directors as the authors of their films. Other theorists believe that movies are best seen as products of a whole society, reflecting values so ingrained that even those who make and view the films are unaware of them. This is the premise of cultural studies.

My approach in this chapter will be to introduce some of the major film theorists and theories chronologically. This is not a comprehensive view, and it necessarily reflects my individual inclinations. I offer it for those who want a sampling of the most influential thoughts and thinkers on the nature of cinema.

Film as Art

Back in the days when motion pictures were still called "photoplays," some notable writers sought to make a case for film as art. In *The Art of the Moving Picture* (1915), Vachel Lindsay explored the basic differences between stage and screen. He noticed the importance in movies of action over words, of setting over acting, of splendor and speed over passion and character. Lindsay's observations were intuitive rather than methodic, the insights of a poet, but his ideas anticipated much of the work carried out by more systematic theorists like Sergei Eisenstein, Siegfried Kracauer, and Marshall McLuhan.

Film as a Reflection of the Mind

A year after Lindsay's book appeared, a German psychologist named Hugo Münsterberg published *The Film: A Psychological Study* (1916). Münsterberg was fascinated by relationships between the public images of photoplays and the imagery of mental life. He regarded the close-up, for example, as analogous to the mental act of attention, a perceptual technique that "has furnished art with a means which far transcends the power of any theater stage" (38). Similarly, he saw the flashback as "an objectification of our memory function" (41). Münsterberg's analysis made serious claims for film's artistic and psychological powers, stressing a point that later critics would elaborate in great detail: Watching movies is not a matter of passive spectatorship, but a mentally engaging act of interpretation.

Russian Formalism

The first comprehensive efforts to develop a theory of film took place not in the United States or Germany, but in Russia. Soon after the Revolution of 1917, the Soviets recognized the power of motion pictures to move the masses. As few cameras were available, the State Film School in Moscow concentrated on the art of editing. Experimenting with existing film footage, Lev Kuleshov showed his students how new meanings result from new arrangements of the images. In one famous experiment, he interspliced close-ups of the actor Ivan Mozhukhin with shots of a coffin, a bowl of soup, and a little girl. At first the students marvelled at Mozhukhin's ability to emote grief, hunger, and compassion. Then they realized that these feelings were not in his face; they were in the viewer's consciousness, influenced by Kuleshov's arrangement of the shots. Vsevolod Pudovkin was among those who learned this lesson well. In *Film Technique* (1926) and *Film Acting* (1935), Pudovkin methodically applied the concept of "relational editing" to show how the sequence of shots can guide the spectator's thinking. Another student of the State Film School, Sergei Eisenstein, took the concept further. In *The Film Sense* (trans. 1947) and *Film Form* (trans. 1949), Eisenstein developed a more dynamic view of editing, what he called "montage." To Eisenstein, the essence of montage was conflict, a dialectic in which *A* collides with *B* to form something entirely new. Drawing on sources as diverse as Chinese ideograms and Hegelian philosophy, Eisenstein fashioned an elaborate system to explain the dynamics of audience response and to guide future filmmakers toward a creative new frontier.

Some Marxists, like the Hungarian theorist Béla Balázs, have also focused on the formal elements of film. In his *Theory of the Film* (1948), Balázs astutely analyzed the close-up, the camera angle, framing, and sound for their emotional impact on the viewer. He also recognized with remarkable clarity the social and economic significance of film. Others have followed other paths. The Hungarian Marxist, George Lukács, was less interested in manipulations of form than in objective reproduction. A realist, he believed that the artist should faithfully record what he sees, "without fear or favor" (Giannetti 1990, 391). One of the most influential Marxist critics, Walter Benjamin, proposed a provocatively historical view of film. In "The Work of Art in the Age of Mechanical Reproduction" (1935), Benjamin argued that motion pictures are the first form of pictorial art to be consumed as products by the masses. Since movies are mechanically reproduced, they satisfy a desire to bring things closer to large audiences for mass consumption. Benjamin explored the political implications of this phenomenon, which he saw as unique in the history of art (Mast and Cohen 1985, 675–94).

The Ideological Approach

Whatever their differences, however, most Marxists view art as an instrument for social change. Films, for them, are always ideological; they embody the value structures in which they are produced. In *Ideology and the Image* (1981), Bill Nichols defines ideology as "the image a society gives of itself in order to perpetuate itself" (1). Because movies are photographic, so like life, they usually obscure the fact that they themselves are constructs and that the values embedded in their images are also constructs. A major function of the Marxist critic, then, is to "demystify" the image, to expose the artifice in cinematic art and remind us that what seems natural and necessary may be only a matter of historical arrangements and therefore can be changed.

Bazin and the Mise-en-Scène Approach

Eisenstein's emphasis on montage editing is often contrasted with the emphasis placed on mise en scène by the French critic, André Bazin. Mise en scène, literally translated as "put into the scene," refers to all the elements in a single shot of film: the action, costumes, framing, camera placement, lenses, and so on. Whereas montage essentially is an arrangement of time, mise en scène is an arrangement of space. Bazin was especially interested in deep-focus photography because it offers a richer space and more closely mirrors the real world. In contrast to rapid montage, it allows the viewer to become more deeply engaged in the film image, to explore its textures and ambiguities. Bazin's essays, collected in *What Is Cinema?* (1967), are concerned with the ability of film to stop the flow of time and hold it in abeyance, in an eternal present tense. For him, "photography does not create eternity, as art does, it embalms time, rescuing it simply from its proper corruption" (14). Cinema—photography in motion—preserves not only the image of things but also the sense of their duration.

German Realists and Antirealists

This ability of film to salvage time is a central issue for Siegfried Kracauer, whose *Theory of Film* (1960) offers a comprehensive analysis of realism in cinema. Like other realists, Kracauer argues that film, because it reproduces reality so well, has an obligation to record it, to reveal it, to "redeem" it. His work is partly a response to the German tradition of expressionism, which he regards as dangerously divorced from the concrete world. In place of a sterile "art for art's sake," he proposes an aesthetically fruitful return to nature.

Rudolf Arnheim's *Film as Art* (1966) represents an opposing, antirealist view. For Arnheim, the power of film is related to its limitations. The goal is not to achieve a more complete picture of reality, but to exploit the very qualities of film which prevent it from being a perfect imitation of life. The fact that motion pictures are two-dimensional, that they are fixed within a rectangular frame, and that they are cut off from the flow of action and edited as shots and scenes are what gives filmmakers the tools they need to make cinema an art.

Structuralism and Semiotics

Increasingly in recent years, film theorists have paid more attention to the arbitrary nature of the moving image, and they have sought to do so in a more systematic fashion. The movement known as *struc-turalism* is often allied with semiotics in an effort to study film with a rigor usually reserved for science. Semiotics is the study of signs and codes. It views cinema, literature, and even clothing as systems of signs that derive their meaning from the conventional structures, or codes, which members of a given society share with other members of that society. The underlying principles of semiotics usually are traced back to the Swiss linguist, Ferdinand de Saussure. Saussure regarded the sign as a unit of relation between a signifier and what it signifies. When we say, "a goat ate my hat," the word *goat* is the signifier while the idea of a goat is the signified. The sign here is neither the spoken nor written word itself, nor the idea behind the word, but a relationship between the two. Semiotics, then, proposes a relational view of language, language as a system of structural affinities. Saussure emphasized that the signifier bears no necessary relation to the signified. Words are arbitrary, artificial, even meaningless. There is no natural reason why the sound represented by the letters *g-o-a-t* should make us think of a four-footed, hairy creature with a beard, just an agreement among English-speaking people—a convention, a code—as is the order of words in a sentence. "A goat ate my hat" is meaningful, while "ate goat hat my a" is not, because it does not follow the code of English syntax. Saussure's ideas and development of semiotics are explained more thoroughly in several useful introductions to the subject, among them Terence Hawkes's *Structuralism and Semiotics* (1977) and Robert Scholes's *Semiotics and Interpretation* (1982).

One of the first to apply these principles to motion pictures was Christian Metz, whose *Film Language* (1968) is a standard text of film semiotics. His analysis of film "language" is more sophisticated than most, though he concludes that the analogy to language can be applied only with great caution. For one thing, notes Metz, film lacks the arbitrariness of natural languages. The signifiers of film—like the photographic image of a goat or the recorded bellow on a sound track—bear a likeness to the signified which words do not. Second, while the order of shots in a film sequence may make a difference in their meaning, the codes for editing are far from being as precise as the codes for syntax. As Metz (1947, 69) observes, "film is a rich message with a poor code." (His effort to formulate this code in a grand syntagm—a universal syntax of film—is described in Chapter 2.) While semioticians have helped to clarify a good many questions of film theory, their efforts to produce a rigorous framework for understanding films have done little to illuminate the films themselves.

Lacan and the Psychoanalytic Approach

Metz himself has turned to other methodologies. In *The Imaginary Signifier* (1977), he looks to psychoanalysis for help in understanding the power of film to hold its audience. Specifically, he draws on the work of French psychoanalyst Jacques Lacan. According to Lacan, the child begins to form a separate identity during the "mirror stage" of its development. Looking in the mirror, the child identifies with its likeness as something other than the image of its mother. It perceives its mirror image as a coherent whole, but as always "over there," as elsewhere. Metz sees the cinema screen as yet another mirror, but one in which the spectator never sees his or her own reflection. With what, then, does the spectator identify? Metz answers: With the pure act of perception. This line of analysis leads deep into post-Freudian territory, linking film spectatorship with voyeurism, exhibitionism, fetishism, and castration anxiety.

For film theory, the special interest in Lacan lies primarily in his emphasis on perception (and misperception) during key moments in the growth of the psyche. Lacan links the infant's scopic drive (its visual curiosity) to pleasure and to early assumptions about its own identity. According to Lacanian film critics, much of the pleasure of watching films can be traced to a childhood desire to peer into forbidden worlds. In the darkness of the theater, the spectator observes people on the screen, but these people can't see the spectator. Spectatorship is thus a form of voyeurism, tinged with erotic longing for the visual object: The movie star becomes a sex object. But the screen is also a reflective medium, as when the spectator identifies with a film performer. In his account of the mirror stage of child development, Lacan points out that the child identifies with its mirror image as something distinct from its mother. There is pleasure in this identification with the image—from it stems the child's first beliefs in bodily coherence— but there is also anxiety. For one thing, the child's reflection looks more complete than the child actually feels itself to be. The belief in bodily coherence is imaginary, based on a false image of self. When the child becomes aware of sexual difference, its earlier narcissistic notions of a full, coherent self give way to dread. This is a time when children entertain menacing ideas about castration to account for the mother's lack of a phallus. In Freudian psychoanalytic theory, the anxiety that accompanies the knowledge of sexual difference is a necessary condition of the Oedipal stage. The male child desires to eliminate his father and secure unrivaled intimacy with his mother. The female child desires the reverse: to achieve union with her father at the mother's expense. Guilty pleasures. In Freudian terms, the child usually adjusts to these conflicts by repressing his or her knowledge and anxieties in the unconscious, thus taking a major step toward becoming a social being. At the same time, the child begins to enter the symbolic world, the linguistic world of signification, becoming forever alienated from the "real" as he or she acquires a cultural identity.

The Feminist Approach

The socializing process, more specifically the male bias in this process, is of special interest to feminists. In her essay, "Recent Developments in Feminist Criticism" (1985), Christine Gledhill begins with the idea that "women as women" are not represented in the cinema. It's not that movies have no female roles, but that these roles too frequently are stereotypes, that they are presented from a male point of view, as an object for men's eyes. In Claire Johnston's words, "within a sexist ideology and a male-dominated cinema, woman is presented as what she represents for man" (Gledhill 1985, 818). The perceptual stance most generally available to viewers is the male gaze. Feminist criticism has drawn from several sources for theoretical support. Semiotics offers a way to look beyond the female stereotypes to the way film texts are composed. It helps to show how what is often taken to be natural, a slice of life, is actually constructed. Like the Marxists, feminists are apt to look for signs of a dominant ideology embedded in the cinematic text. By recognizing patriarchal structures in a film, feminists believe the educated viewer can resist being taken in.

Laura Mulvey's essay on "Visual Pleasure and Narrative Cinema" (Mast 1985, 803) uses psychoanalytic theory as a political weapon, examining the language of patriarchy with its own tools. She argues that the female figure on the screen is fashioned for men's visual pleasure, that the way she is to be looked at is built into the spectacle itself, that the audience is unwittingly stitched into the fiction. The glamorized actress, isolated on the screen, is a sexual icon on display for the male protagonist and the male spectator. She is the bearer, not the maker of meaning. But Mulvey finds a contradiction in the play of voyeurism, fetishism, and castration fears within this cinematic structure. This study of Alfred Hitchcock and Josef Von Sternberg is a classic, setting a tone and level of complexity for more than a decade of feminist thought.

Derrida and Deconstruction

Metz and Lacan are two of the most important recent European influences on American film theory. The impact of French philosopher Jacques Derrida has been less direct. Derrida's influence on literary studies, generally associated with the term *deconstruction,* is described by Christopher Norris in *Deconstruction: Theory & Practice* (1982). Norris presents deconstruction as a reaction to structuralism. Where structuralists read texts for the universal structures of meaning corresponding to deep-seated patterns of mind, Derrida and his followers show that no structure can account for all the elements of a text, and that all structures ultimately undo themselves through self-contradiction. Derrida defies the very idea of classification, challenging the foundations of Western thought.

Derrida argues that concepts traditionally considered whole and complete within themselves—like truth and nature—actually rely on opposite concepts (falsehood, culture) for their meaning. For example, the idea of good is meaningless without the idea of evil. Derrida shows that each concept contains a "trace" of its opposite, contaminating its presumed purity, contradicting the logical principle of unity. Derrida's analysis of texts typically identifies a contradiction in some key term (like the word *pharmakon* in Plato, which means both poison and remedy) or unconscious rhetorical strategy (like Rousseau's metaphor of writing as supplement). These are the "blind spots" which reveal a text's instability, its resistance to being defined or reduced to any final concept. The work of deconstruction, says Norris, is to read texts radically, "not so much for their interpretive 'insights' as for the symptoms of 'blindness' which mark their conceptual limits" (1982, 23).

Derrida's approach has been most persuasively applied to film by Peter Brunette and David Wills in *Screen/Play: Derrida and Film Theory* (1989). Brunette and Wills use Derrida to critique contemporary film theory. They demonstrate how the "essentializing gestures" of film history and genre theory always require some form of exclusion. Any effort to speak broadly about German expressionism or the Hollywood film, about Westerns or film noir, represses differences within each category as well as similarities between categories. The paradox of studying film by means of genre, history, or any other generalizing principle is that the number of common traits constituting any group is exceeded by the number of uncommon traits or by the number of traits shared across group boundaries. Thus deconstruction offers a critique of structuralist readings which view film texts as exemplars of some class or formula. Brunette and Wills move beyond the deconstructionist critique in Chapter Five, where they offer experimental readings, based on Derridean ideas, of two fascinating films, François Truffaut's *The Bride Wore Black* (1968) and David Lynch's *Blue Velvet* (1986).

Brunette and Wills face a problem which Derrida himself acknowledged: How do you analyze contradictions of language if language is your chief tool of analysis? How do you expose the blind spots in a text without being blind to your own? Derrida proposes several conceptual strategies. One has been called *erasure*, a process by which words are treated as if they were crossed out as soon as they are written. An X through each key word reminds the reader that no term can be taken at face value. Words are necessary but provisional rungs on a ladder that is dismantled one step behind its own construction. Another strategy is enacted in the term *différance*, which in French combines two senses: "to differ" and "to defer," thus fusing space and time. Language is constituted by difference because it is by oppositions that we distinguish meaning, as Saussure had pointed out. But meaning is also always deferred, because there is always a surplus of meaning in the play of signification within a text. The meaning of the term différance is itself provisional, fashioned by the difference between differ and defer and thus perpetually deferred.

Derrida is not just playing games—his studies are meticulously analytical—but his commitment to subverting single-minded readings of any text must be applied to his readings as well. The work of deconstruction is an endless struggle to erase its own traces, to avoid getting entangled in the contradictions it elucidates. Continually questioning its own grounds, it never rests.

And so the work of film theory keeps moving on.

Further Readings

I began by saying that this chapter would be more of a sampling than a summary of film theories. For a more thorough, detailed survey of the field, there are several respected studies and anthologies.

A standard collection of key readings is *Movies and Methods* (1976), edited by Bill Nichols. Nichols draws together an intriguing variety of criticism and theory, ranging from François Truffaut and Susan Sontag to Raymond Durgnat and Stephen Koch. The essays are divided into political criticism, genre criticism, feminist criticism, auteur criticism, mise-en-scène criticism, film theory, and structuralist semiology, reflecting what Nichols considers to be the key critical methodologies of the seventies.

Another popular anthology is *Film Theory and Criticism,* edited by Gerald Mast and Marshall Cohen. The third edition (1985) spans the field from Münsterberg to Metz and beyond. Mast and Cohen frame the issues in seven categories: Film and Reality; Film Image and Film Language; The Film Medium; Film, Theater, and Literature; Film Genres; The Film as Art; and Film: Psychology, Society, and Ideology. Their prefaces to each section are clear and concise, useful guideposts by which to steer a beginning course through the shifting currents of film theory.

One of the earliest (and still one of the clearest) introductions to film theory is by Dudley Andrew. In *The Major Film Theories* (1976), Andrew offers a critical survey of the first five decades, outlining the broad movements of formalism, realism, and contemporary French semiology and phenomenology. He analyzes eight major theorists along Aristotelian lines, comparing their views on the raw material of film, its methods and techniques, its forms and shapes, its purposes and values. His book provides an orderly map of the field as it appeared in the mid-seventies.

Andrew turns to more recent developments in *Concepts in Film Theory* (1984), noting that modern film theory is no longer organized around individual theorists, but pirouettes around key concepts. Andrew organizes his book around several conceptual hubs, including perception, representation, signification, valuation, identification, and figuration. He outlines the arguments between realists and perceptual psychologists, between genre and auteur critics, between psychoanalytic and cultural camps, noting how contemporary thinking on film is tied to other intellectual movements. "In sum," he says, "film theory today consists primarily in thinking through, elaborating, and critiquing the key metaphors by which we seek to understand (and control) the cinema complex" (1984, 12).

Philip Rosen has sought to clarify the complex tissue of modern film theory in somewhat different terms. His anthology of theoretical texts, *A Film Theory Reader* (1986), divides the field into issues of narrative (structures of cinematic storytelling), subject positioning (the psychology of film spectatorship), apparatus (film technology), and ideology (cultural politics). Rosen offers an analysis of the shift from structuralist interests in cinematic patterns to post-structuralist interests in the dynamics of process. He also points out the dilemma of feminists who rely on Lacan's patriarchal terms for their criticism and thus struggle to find alternative representations. Finally, he interrogates the machinery of cinema, asking what ideological biases operate within the apparatus. The theorists whom he includes go beyond simple technological determinism to explore the cultural determinants at work in the technology. Reading Rosen's introductory chapters is one way to decipher the enigmatic terms encountered in modern film theory, terms like *symbolization, signification, subject, pleasure, suture, lack, excess,* and *imaginary signifier.*

6 Film in the English Class

As early as 1911, when the National Council of Teachers of English was founded, English teachers recognized the educational significance of motion pictures. Dale Adams has traced the shifting tides of film study within the profession from the first days of condescending skepticism to more recent signs of its acceptance in the schools (Costanzo 1987, 3–7). In the 1920s and 1930s, NCTE was primarily concerned with raising standards of film appreciation and arming students with critical perspectives. After World War II, when movies were considered merely one of several "visual aids," and during the Sputnik era, when movies were regarded as diversions from the national agenda, film study declined in popularity. It was not until the 1970s that a fresh wave of media awareness found its way into the schools, inspired by creative trends in European cinema, fostered by visionary critics like Marshall McLuhan and Andrew Sarris, and sustained by a young generation of enthusiastic teachers who discovered how to apply their literary training to the new discipline of film. Today, after several steps "back to basics" in the early 1980s, the study of film seems to be growing once again, supported by advances in technology and strengthened by developments in theory and experience.

Film is studied differently in different settings. In colleges and universities, the trend is to treat film as a separate discipline. In *The American Film Institute Guide to College Courses in Film and Television* (1978), Bohnenkamp and Grogg list over 1,000 institutions of higher learning in the United States which together offer more than 9,000 courses in film and television. The Modern Language Association's *Film Study in the Undergraduate Curriculum* (Grant 1983) highlights representative practices and programs ranging from a one-faculty initiative at the University of Chicago to some 950 students enrolled in film courses at the University of Illinois at Urbana-Champaign. College courses include Film Appreciation; Film History; Film Genres; Great Directors; Literature and Film; Thematic Studies (Images of Women, War on Film); and interdisciplinary offerings (Cinema and Society, Science and Film). In secondary schools, film study tends to be more restricted. According to Joan Lynch (1983), film is an accepted part of the curriculum for many English teachers, and most high schools do offer a film course, but the offerings are supplemental, peripheral, and rarely integrated into the curriculum. Elsewhere, Lynch finds that most high school and elementary school teachers use films to stimulate thematic discussions or to clarify literary concepts. They are more likely to teach film as literature than film as film (Costanzo 1987, 9).

A Selection of Approaches

How are movies being used in the schools? Teachers have developed film courses in a variety of ways for a variety of purposes. Here are some examples from a panel of college instructors who teach outside departments of film studies. The panel was organized for the Society for Cinema Studies Conference in 1987.

Linda Dittmar teaches a course on "Women Film Directors" at the University of Massachusetts, Boston. Her syllabus includes *The Blue Light* (Leni Riefenstahl, 1932), *Marianne and Juliane* (Margarethe von Trotta, 1981), *Meshes of the Afternoon* (Deren, 1943), *Namibia* (Choy, 1985), *Amy* (Vincent McEveety, 1981), and *Born in Flames* (Borden, 1983).

Angela Vacche teaches "Italian Cinema" at Vassar College to introduce students to Italian history and culture. She alternates lectures on Italian painting, Futurism, Fascism, neorealism, and contemporary culture with screenings of films like *Umberto D* (Vittorio De Sica, 1952), *La Notte* (Michelangelo Antonioni, 1961), *Satyricon* (Federico Fellini, 1969), *The Tree of the Wooden Clogs* (Ermanno Olmi, 1978), and *Chaos* (the Taviani brothers, 1985).

Steve Lipkin teaches an introductory course called "Film Communication" at Western Michigan University. The course acquaints students with the language, technology, and aesthetics of film through investigations of films like *Meet John Doe* (Frank Capra, 1941), *Casablanca* (Michael Curtiz, 1943), *Potemkin* (Sergei Eisenstein, 1925), *Stagecoach* (John Ford, 1939), and *McCabe and Mrs. Miller* (Robert Altman, 1971).

Harriet Margolis teaches a course in "Gender, Race, and Communication" at Florida Atlantic University. Books by Angela Davis, Maxine Hong Kingston, and Fred MacDonald are combined with films like *Prelude to War* (Frank Capra, 1941), *Black Girl* (Ossie Davis, 1972), *Imitation of Life* (John M. Stahl, 1934), and *Small Happiness: Women of a Chinese Village* (Hinton and Gordon, 1984).

Kevin Sweeney teaches "Film Aesthetics" at the University of Tampa, exploring issues of contemporary philosophy through films like *The General* (Buster Keaton, 1926), *The Bicycle Thief* (Vittorio De Sica, 1948), and *Hiroshima Mon Amour* (Alain Resnais, 1959).

Jeff Hendricks teaches a course called "Femininity/Masculinity in the Cinema" at Centenary College of Louisiana. He combines readings by Freud, traditional film critics, and feminist theorists with screenings of films like *Blonde Venus* (Josef Von Sternberg, 1932), *The Searchers* (John Ford, 1956), *Women in Love* (Ken Russell, 1969), *Daughter Rite* (Citron, 1978), *Sugarbaby* (Percy Adlon, 1985), and *Pumping Iron* (George Butler, 1977).

Robin Bates and Michael Berger teach a course called "Technology and the American Dream." Films like *Modern Times* (Charles Chaplin, 1936), *The War of the Worlds* (Byron Haskin, 1952), and *A Clockwork Orange* (Stanley Kubrick, 1971) are paired with readings by Mark Twain, Ralph Ellison, Ursula LeGuin, and Susan Sontag on America's preoccupation with technology.

Lester Friedman of Syracuse University teaches *Gentleman's Agreement* (Elia Kazan, 1947), *The Pawnbroker* (Sidney Lumet, 1965), *Hester Street* (Joan Micklin Silver, 1974), *Annie Hall* (Woody Allen, 1977), and *The Chosen* (Jeremy Paul Kagan, 1981) as examples of "Jewish-American Cinema."

Shoshana Knapp teaches a course on "Literature and Film" at Virginia Polytechnic Institute, where she compares film adaptations like *A Farewell to Arms* (Charles Vidor, 1957), *The Go-Between* (Joseph Losey, 1970), *The Third Man* (Carol Reed, 1949), and *The Killers* (Don Siegel, 1964) to the original stories.

Diane Carson teaches a course on "Science Fiction Films" at St. Louis Community College. The course includes *The Woman in the Moon* (Fritz Lang, 1929), *Metropolis* (Fritz Lang, 1926), *Forbidden Planet* (Fred M. Wilcox, 1956), *Fantastic Voyage* (Richard Fleischer, 1966), *2001: A Space Odyssey* (Stanley Kubrick, 1968), and *Alien* (Ridley Scott, 1979).

Sharon Strom teaches a course called "America on Screen" at the University of Rhode Island. She uses films like *Scarface* (Howard Hawks, 1932), *Birth of a Nation* (D. W. Griffith, 1915), *The Grapes of Wrath* (John Ford, 1940), *On the Waterfront* (Elia Kazan, 1954), and *Footlight Parade* (Lloyd Bacon, 1933) to focus on key moments in American history.

Instead of creating separate courses in film, some teachers integrate films into their regular classes. The following examples are culled from

"Film Study in English Classes," an unpublished survey by the NCTE Committee on Film Study in 1986:

Ann Dobie (University of Southwestern Louisiana) uses films to illustrate composing principles, structuring devices, and rhetorical strategies that are also used by writers.

Thelma Shenkel (Baruch College) has students read Orwell's *1984* in conjunction with films on totalitarianism.

Frank Masiello (New York City Technical College) discusses recent motion pictures dealing with family relationships, sexuality, racism, and other contemporary themes.

Vera Jiji (Brooklyn College) has students screen films like *Uncle Tom's Cabin* as primary material for research on historical topics.

Norah Chase (Kingsborough Community College) introduces feminist literature together with documentary films on women. Students then interview women in their families and neighborhoods as part of their research.

One of the most innovative—and enduring—programs of film study in secondary schools has been led by Ralph Amelio at Willowbrook High School near Chicago. The Willowbrook Cinema Study Project has been a model program since the 1960s. Based on a firm foundation of goals, methods, and evaluation, it still has been flexible enough to change its content and emphasis with the times. In *Film in the Classroom* (1971), Amelio outlines ten units of instruction, with suggested films, readings, and activities. The units include Film and Literature; Film Language; Comedy: Old and New; The Adolescent; The Documentary; Animation; War; Art and Fantasy; The Western and Myth; and On Style: The Director and The Actor. More recently, Amelio's course has focused on the Vietnam experience, drawing on films like *The Deer Hunter* (1978) and *Apocalypse Now* (1979). Amelio notes that his students work hard, possibly harder than in any other high school course. In their course evaluations, they attribute their effort to a sense of serious involvement with important issues. "They realized," Amelio concludes, "that not only could film record reality but from reality it could make art that humanized and liberated them from their restricted world of 'me-them' into a world of discovery, sensitivity, and seeing" (1971, 126).

Activities for Class and Home

How does such discovery take place? What actually happens in the classroom?

One difference between film courses and other subjects is that the films are often screened in class, whereas novels, plays, and other texts are usually read outside of class. Fitting a two-hour feature film into standard fifty-minute periods can be a challenge. Screening a film in two consecutive classes disrupts its continuity and takes away from valuable discussion time. For this reason, some film classes are scheduled in longer time-blocks or special screenings are arranged outside of class. Now that many films are available on videocassette, it is becoming possible to assign movies like books, to be viewed individually at home or in a section of the library equipped with VCRs. Still, many teachers feel that the experience of watching films as they were intended to be shown—on a large screen with a large audience—is worth the extra effort to preserve class screenings.

Discussion is often the heart of class. It pumps up the mental energy, gets the juices flowing, circulates ideas, and nourishes the group's collective insight. Discussing a film enables students to articulate their personal experiences, to compare their first impressions to other points of view, to connect what they have seen to larger social, political, and cultural events. A good discussion also clarifies the facts, establishing boundaries between what was seen and what was imagined, between private reactions and cultural norms. The tenor of discussion can be factual: What happened in the movie? What did you see and hear? It can be personal: How did you feel during each scene? What was going through your mind? It can be contextual: How did this remind you of other movies, other scenes, other moments in art or life? The discussion can be analytic, focusing on specific elements within the film that contributed to a given effect. It can be evaluative, with students judging how well the effect was achieved. Or it can be dialectic, with students taking sides on a given issue.

Before screening the film, if often helps to give a brief introduction. Students may want to know about the historical context of *The Grapes of Wrath,* or the musical tradition that preceded *Singin' in the Rain,* or Orson Welles's career before he directed *Citizen Kane.* Handouts describing the film's production team and cast are also useful, as are excerpts from film reviews, lists of related films, and bibliographies. These may serve as prompts for the discussion and guides to student projects.

Teachers have varied the pattern of introduction, screening, and discussion depending on the film. Sometimes it makes sense to show the entire film before discussion. Sometimes it seems best to stop the film at several points, discussing students' expectations and assumptions before moving on. When time permits, a key scene may be screened again during discussion. This enables students to do a close textual reading, applying their analysis inductively to the film as a whole. Some teachers have experimented with the technical features of a film. They show a scene without the sound track, asking students what sounds they imagine; they play the sound track without the picture, asking students to visualize the scene. Some teachers have their students read the script or story first, then compare it to the film experience. Others show an adaptation before reading the original to make it clearer how a filmed interpretation affects the reader's imagination.

Responses to the film do not always take the form of a discussion. Sometimes students write down their immediate reactions. Sometimes they complete questionnaires, then pool the results to form a class profile. The class response may be in the form of role-playing (with students imagining new situations for the characters), panels (with different students concentrating on camera work, directing, sound, or other elements of the film), or an original film (with students filming their own local adaptation or sequel to the film).

My own inclination is to let students take more responsibility for the introduction and discussion through group presentations. After I lead several classes, students sign up in groups of two to four for one of the remaining films on the syllabus. Each group prepares introductory material and discussion questions. During the class session, they present the film and lead the discussion. In this way, they have a chance to study one film in depth, screening it together, investigating the background, sampling reviews, and learning about the principal artists, technicians, and performers. They also have a chance to practice public speaking skills. What I find is that the prospect of a performance before peers draws out even the most withdrawn of students. With some tactful guidance and enough time to prepare, they become the class experts on at least one film. Their research and their study questions become part of the course content, a fact that contributes to the quality of research and discussion. And since all students get a turn, their responsiveness to one another tends to be high. The oral presentation is described more completely in Appendix 2.

Individual and group projects may take many forms. Ralph Amelio describes students who responded most creatively to film. One talented young woman wrote, scored, and played an original mood piece in response to her favorite film unit. Another student took photographs and mounted them in a collage, which he unified with an original poem. A third student used a movie camera to film hundreds of photographs in quick succession, adding an original sound track to express his response to a unit on violence in society (1971, 63–64). More traditional assignments include film comparisons and film reviews.

In a film comparison, students compare one film from the syllabus to another film. The second film may be a current release or an earlier film that bears some relationship worth exploring. For example, the original *King Kong* (1933) might be paired with one of its many sequels. *The Blackboard Jungle* (1955) might be matched with *Stand and Deliver* (1987) or another film about city schools. Two films by the same director or featuring the same performer might be studied side by side for what they reveal about his or her artistic style and growth.

A film review is an opportunity to apply what students learn in class to a fresh film experience. They might begin by reading and reporting on several reviews of a new film culled from different sources. This acquaints them with the form and scope of film reviews. Or they may write an original review of a contemporary film. It is sometimes entertaining and enlightening to hear from student reviewers who take different views of the same film.

Three additional projects are described in Appendix 2. The "Shot-by-Shot Analysis" involves students in a close reading of one scene. They examine the technical elements in each shot, then see how those elements contribute to the broader meanings of the scene. "Behind the Scenes" gives students a chance to investigate one aspect of filmmaking in depth: directing, acting, script writing, photography, music, set design. By looking behind the scenes of a particular film to the work of a particular technician or performer, they learn about the craft as well as the art of filmmaking. "Fiction into Film" is a more ambitious venture. Here students get involved in all stages of film production, from scripting to editing. They begin by selecting a short story or poem for adaptation to the screen. Then they scout locations, cast the characters, and prepare a storyboard or shooting script outlining each scene. If there is time to film the script, a production crew does the shooting, editing, and sound track. Not only does the group learn about moviemaking through hands-on experience; it also learns about the intricacies of adaptation. In the process, students learn to pay close attention to the details of a narrative. In transforming settings into actual locations, characters into a cast, description into action, or tone and point of view into photography and sound, they become involved in literature—and cinema—as never before (see Costanzo 1985 for a more complete discussion of this approach).

Equipment and Resources

Projection equipment is no longer the impediment it used to be. As recently as 1983, the MLA publication on film study echoed a familiar lament that "because of the nature of the medium, it is impossible without access to special equipment (analytic projectors, moviolas) to engage in a close textual analysis of film" (Grant 1983, ix). Today, anyone with access to a videocassette or videodisk player can quickly scan backwards or forwards through a film, play a scene in slow motion, or freeze a single frame. No longer must viewers rely on photographic memories and notes scribbled in the dark. Film texts can be studied with the same deliberate concentration that scholars and students have given to literary texts. No longer must they rely on theatrical screenings or TV's Million Dollar Movie to see a certain film. With thousands of titles available in video format, and hundreds more on cable television, films can be selected like books. What's more, specific moments of a film can be selected like any literary passage and viewed repeatedly.

Videodisk technology is best suited for this kind of selective viewing because any frame can be projected instantly by keying in its reference number by remote control. This allows a film class to jump from frame to frame, comparing the acting or lighting in one scene to comparable elements in another scene, or to advance the film one frame at a time, disclosing the mysteries of animation or fine points of editing. At last it's possible to see how Orson Welles achieved that extraordinary crane shot through the skylight of the El Rancho nightclub in *Citizen Kane* or how King Kong interacts with Faye Wray.

On a videodisk, each frame is represented by a groove. Since the information in a groove is digital, stored as tiny pits, it is less susceptible to wear than the analog information of celluloid film or videocassette. This results in images and sound that retain their sharpness through repeated use. Normally, the laser reads one groove at a time while the disk spins underneath, much as a conventional record. Sequential projection of twenty-four frames per second produces the continuity of motion pictures. A still frame is produced by stopping the laser over a single groove. Since this has no effect on the groove itself, the frame can be projected indefinitely. No holes are burned in the middle of the film, no scan lines flutter in the frame.

Videodisks are also useful because they interact well with computers. A few years ago, I connected my school's videodisk player to an Apple computer so that students could control films projected on a video monitor from the computer's keyboard. A simple program in BASIC enabled me to present questions about the film on the computer screen. Students used the keyboard both to regulate the scene and to answer the questions. At the end of a session, they could reproduce their answers on a printer. The computer even rearranged the results of their analysis into a shot-by-shot printout of the action, angle, camera movement, lighting, sound, and transitions. Today there are ready-made computer programs offering more sophisticated features, like the University of Pennsylvania's CINEMA project. CINEMA includes study questions and a textual database about films that are available on laserdisks. This means that students can control the moving image, background information, and their writing on the same computer screen.

Respecting Copyright Laws

When teachers were limited to 16mm films, there was little risk of violating copyright laws. The great majority of 16mm prints were legally purchased or rented by the schools; for the most part, it was technically unfeasible to copy them. With the advent of VCRs, however, the technical options have increased, as have the legal issues. It is relatively easy to copy movies off the air, but is it lawful to show the copies to a class? Inexpensive films on videotape can now be bought or rented for home viewing, but can they be shown legally in school? Technology is changing so rapidly that the courts can barely keep pace. While interpretations differ and the legal terms are not always clear, any teacher who shows movies in the classroom should be aware of copyright restrictions. This section is an introduction to the basics.

Under the Copyright Act of 1976, authors are protected against unauthorized copying of original works. The intent, in keeping with the Constitution, is to benefit the public as well as the author. Copyright protection is presumed to promote the production of books, music, films, and other works which contribute to public knowledge and intellectual pursuits (U.S. Congress Office of Technology Assessment 1989, 5). By guaranteeing the right of authors to profit from their work, the law seeks to encourage work that serves the general good. Works created after January 1, 1978 are now automatically protected for fifty years after the author's death, and the law applies to earlier works as well. After this protection period, works fall into the "public domain"; then the restriction no longer applies (Sinofsky 1984, 39).

The Copyright Act of 1976 does not set precise limits for using new technologies like videocassettes. Nor does it offer detailed guidelines for fields like education. It does, however, allow copying for certain purposes under the category of "fair use." Fair use, described in Section 107 of the new act, permits special exemptions for education, criticism, scholarship, and similar reasons (Sinofsky 1984, 115). It is a kind of "escape clause" which, like any legal concept, is subject to testing in the courts.

To date, two important cases have helped to define the limits of fair use. One case began in 1978 when several film distributors sued the New York State Board of Cooperative Educational Services (BOCES) for taping hundreds of movies off the air and distributing copies to public schools. The court ruled that such large-scale, systematic videotaping was illegal, even for educational purposes. A key point of the decision was that most of the movies were available for purchase or rental. The financial harm to copyright owners was judged to be more important than the convenience to schools of copying these movies off the air (Sinofsky 1984, 68–78). The second case began in 1979, when Sony was sued for manufacturing its Betamax machine on the grounds that this permitted users to tape copyrighted material off the air. Sony took the case all the way to the Supreme Court. While the Court ruled in Sony's favor, its 1984 decision applied primarily to home use for the purpose of "time shifting"—taping material to be viewed at a more convenient time (Sinofsky 1984, 78–88). The implications for teachers remained largely unsettled.

In the absence of precise criteria, Congress has sought standards of fair use. A committee appointed by Congressman Robert Kastenmeier in May of 1979 suggested a set of guidelines for education. While these guidelines do not have the force of law, they represent a serious governmental effort to set standards for taping off the air (Sinofsky 1984, 119–20). Who decides to do the copying is a factor in these guidelines. An individual teacher in a nonprofit school who decides to copy something from television to use in class has a better case than someone who is asked to do the copying by the school administration (Miller 1979, 13). The key concept here is "spontaneity": If it is not feasible to rent or purchase certain material in time for a teachable moment, it may be fair to copy the material. By contrast, stockpiling copied tapes just because they may prove useful in the classroom someday is not considered fair use.

Another factor is how and where copies are displayed. Section 110 of the Copyright Act specifies that a copy be displayed during a face-to-face teaching activity in a regular classroom (Miller 1979, 59). Sending students to the library to see copied tapes on their own may not meet this criterion.

In addition, any copy should be temporary. After its use in the classroom, it should be erased or destroyed. The Kastenmeier committee recommended that off-the-air recordings may be kept for up to forty-five days. It specified that such copies could be used once in class and repeated only for instructional reinforcement. Copies should include the program's copyright notice and not be altered in any way.

To summarize, the law on copyright is still in the process of being applied specifically to technologies like television broadcasting and videocassettes. Although the concept of fair use allows some flexibility for educational uses of films and off-the-air programs, the limits of fair use are subject to interpretation and testing in the courts. It is a good idea to keep in mind the spirit as well as the letter of the law:

1. The intent of copyright legislation is to prevent loss of income to copyright owners. Taping should not be a way to avoid renting or buying a film; if it is feasible to buy or rent it for classroom use, it probably should not be copied.

2. Just because it's technically feasible to copy something doesn't mean it's lawful, even for educational purposes.

3. Many schools have a policy on copyright. Consult your media specialist, district office, or library for local guidelines.

Dealing with Censorship

Censorship has always been a serious concern of teachers, especially English teachers. In a society where education is traditionally viewed as serving public needs, the schools have been subjected throughout history to public pressures. During the early 1970s, when non-print media began to be used more widely in classrooms, Ken Donelson (1973) warned that audio-visual materials were coming under the same kind of attack that novels, textbooks, and other printed forms had undergone for years (1226). An NCTE survey of censorship in 1977 confirmed this, revealing that people were complaining about certain films and AV materials being shown in the schools. Among the films were John Boorman's *Deliverance* (1972), Arthur Penn's *Bonnie and Clyde* (1967), Larry Yust's *The Lottery* (1969), and Franco Zeffirelli's *Romeo and Juliet* (1968). In most cases, the complaints came from parents, and to a lesser extent from school staff, who cited violence, sexual references, offensive language, and unacceptable ideas as their chief objections (Burress 1979, 31–34).

Dealing with censorship requires some understanding of the motives behind it. Robert Small (1979) articulates the view of parents who believe that since they pay for the schools and send their children to them, they ought to have a say in what is taught. Small points out that efforts to censor the curriculum often grow out of a sense of frustration by communities who feel powerless to defend their deeply held beliefs. He cites a sign carried by protestors during the famous 1974 censorship campaign in Kanawha County, West Virginia: "Even hillbillies have rights." These protesting citizens, Small observes, "are to a very considerable extent fulfilling the role assigned to them by the historical development of the American school" (61). Robert Hogan (1979) enlarges this perspective. Hogan agrees that much of the drive to limit schools comes from a basic distrust of those who set the educational agenda. He asks teachers to consider whether they can trust their own agendas. "The uncomfortable truth," he says, is that "we are all censors. The difference is that when English teachers practice censorship, we call it 'book selection' " (88).

Many of the arguments against school censorship are also rooted in American history. Chief among these is the argument for intellectual freedom, traditionally linked to the First Amendment. Edward Jenkinson (1979) expresses this view when he says, "I hope that my children will not have to grow up in a society in which they are denied the right to study any subject, to read any book they deem worthy of attention, and to speak out on any topic they think worthy of discussion" (12). Another argument questions the claim of censors that objectionable works may be harmful to young minds. Reviewing the research on reading, Richard Beach (1979) concludes that books rarely change people's attitudes because "the relatively stable and defined characteristics of readers shape the experience with a work to a greater extent than the work affects characteristics of the reader" (144). Beach extends his observations to visual material, finding no significant evidence that exposure to obscenity changes the viewer's attitudes toward sex or violence. On the contrary, he cites studies suggesting that "erotica is generally beneficial to adolescents' normal sexual development" (151).

Given such arguments and pressures, what can teachers do about selecting films for study and justifying their selection? Many of the steps suggested by Ken Donelson (1979) to handle censorship of print media in the 1970s can help to deal with censorship of visual media in the 1990s. First, develop a departmental rationale statement for teaching film. By supporting your educational objectives with clear, convincing reasons, you strengthen your case for including any film that helps your students realize those objectives. Rationales for specific films can further reinforce your case. Second, set up a committee to recommend film titles. By discussing films that might best suit your students and objectives, you create opportunities to predict potential problems and to anticipate solutions. Third, cultivate community understanding and support before censorship becomes an issue. Parents and public groups are less likely to act on partial information if they have an accurate, full picture in advance. Fourth, encourage your school to form a policy on censorship if it does not already have one. Threats become less urgent when procedures are worked out ahead of time (162–67). Donelson's suggestions underline the value of thoughtful preparation. Prevention is the most expedient way to settle conflict.

II Twelve Great Films on Video

7 Citizen Kane

Produced and directed by Orson Welles; screenplay by Herman J. Mankiewicz and Orson Welles; photography by Gregg Toland; art direction by Van Nest Polglase; set decoration by Darrell Silvera; special effects by Vernon Walker; editing by Robert Wise; music by Bernard Herrmann; released by RKO in 1941. [119 minutes]

Charles Foster Kane	*Orson Welles*
Jedediah Leland	*Joseph Cotten*
Bernstein	*Everett Sloane*
Susan Alexander	*Dorothy Comingore*
James W. Gettys	*Ray Collins*
Jerry Thompson	*William Alland*
Mary Kane	*Agnes Moorehead*
Emily Monroe Norton	*Ruth Warrick*
Walter Thatcher	*George Coulouris*
Herbert Carter	*Erskine Sanford*
Raymond	*Paul Stewart*
Kane, aged 8	*Buddy Swan*

There are good reasons for starting with *Citizen Kane*. It is probably on more lists of "the top ten movies of all time" than any other film. It is consistently cited in the film textbooks and in film courses around the country for its artistry, technique, and themes. Some critics, like Peter Cowie, see it as "a treasury of cinematic metaphors and devices" (1973, 52), while others believe, with David Bordwell, that "the best way to understand *Citizen Kane* is to stop worshipping it as a triumph of technique" and focus on the artistic ends served by these means (Gottesman 1976, 103). A class could devote weeks to *Citizen Kane* without exhausting what it has to offer.

The briefest summary suggests why this is no ordinary film. It begins with the last moments of a dying man, then cuts abruptly from his private sanctuary to the public image projected in a booming newsreel, "News on the March!" A reporter is assigned to uncover the story behind Charles Foster Kane's final word, "Rosebud," and for most of the film we follow the reporter as he pieces together several versions of Kane's life. There is a diary left by Mr. Thatcher, Kane's legal guardian. There are interviews with Bernstein, Kane's deferential business partner; with Leland, his closest friend; with Susan Alexander, his second wife; and with Raymond, his butler. Each version yields more information and another point of view, but what do they add up to? Thompson, the reporter, fails to see what only the objective camera sees as it sniffs through Kane's possessions before leaving the estate, pulling back to the "No Tresspassing" sign on the gate which it had entered in the first shots of the film.

How do we read a life? How do we read a film? *Citizen Kane* invites us to examine our assumptions about interpreting reality and fiction. Which readings are most telling, most convincing? How do we negotiate conflicting points of view? What do we rely on to fill in the gaps between the frames?

The origin of the film itself is entangled in controversy. Critic Pauline Kael (1971) challenged Welles's claims of authorship, contending that most of the credit, from conception to the shooting script, was owed to writer Herman Mankiewicz. Andrew Sarris strongly disagreed (Gottesman 1976, 29). So did Peter Bogdanovich, who drew on taped interviews with Welles to dispute Kael's claims (Gottesman 1976, 28–53). More recently, Robert Carringer (1985) has entered the dispute, emerging with a view of Mankiewicz as author of the story frame, the characters, a few scenes, and some dialogue, but attributing the "narrative brilliance—the visual and verbal wit, the stylistic fluidity" to Welles (35). Carringer makes a carefully documented case for collective authorship. He cites the contributions of Gregg Toland, Welles's director of photography, who helped to plan and execute many of the striking cinematic effects—the long takes, the extraordinary depth of field, elaborate camera movements, low-hung ceilings, and chiaroscuro lighting—the visual hallmarks of the film. He also gives appreciative credit to Bernard Herrmann for the film's memorable score. Herrmann used two musical leitmotifs, which he associated with the themes of power and of Rosebud, to trace Kane's quest for control and love.

The figure of Kane is loosely based on William Randolph Hearst, the newspaper magnate who constructed a private castle in San Simeon, California. In 1918, Hearst fell in love with the movie starlet, Marion Davies, married her, and built a movie studio to further her career. When Hearst learned about the film, he offered RKO $842,000 to burn the print and threatened the entire film industry in his press (Cowie, 1973, 24). After much delay, *Citizen Kane* was screened on May 1, 1941, and it was critically acclaimed. But it was not a financial success, resulting in a loss of $150,000. Yet nothing by Orson Welles before or since has ever matched the achievements of *Citizen Kane.*

Seemingly from birth, Orson Welles (1915–1985) showed a genius for all things theatrical. At the age of four, he was writing, producing, and directing plays for his family. Educated at home until his mother died when he was eight, he spent the next two years touring the world with his entrepreneur father, entering The Todd School in Woodstock, Illinois, when he was ten. Until he graduated at the age of fifteen, Welles spent most of his time acting and directing schoolboy theatricals. At fifteen, his father died, and Welles became the ward of Dr. Maurice Bernstein, a Chicago physician. That summer, with aspirations to become a painter, he went on a sketching holiday to Ireland, and when he ran short of money, he talked himself into an acting berth with The Gate repertory theatre in Dublin.

When the teenager returned to America nine months later, he failed to find an acting job immediately. He tried his hand at playwrighting, illustrating, and mounting summer stock productions before joining Katherine Cornell's repertory company, making his Broadway debut in 1934. An introduction to John Houseman led to his participation in "The March of Time" series on radio—a medium Welles was to make his own during the thirties and forties. His reputation as a *wunderkind* was taking hold.

Houseman and Welles continued their collaboration, first mounting shows for the Federal Theater Project, then with the Mercury Theatre, which became renowned for its innovative Broadway and radio productions. On Halloween eve, 1938, Welles became notorious when he dramatized *The War of the Worlds* on radio as if it were a news broadcast and panicked thousands on the Eastern seaboard. Welles was twenty-three years old.

A child prodigy's performance is a hard act to follow. In 1939, Welles signed a contract with RKO to write, produce, direct, and star in several films. *Citizen Kane* was the first of these, but it was also the last film on which he had complete creative control until *The Trial* some twenty years later. His gracefully nostalgic *The Magnificent Ambersons* (1942) and the spy thriller *Journey into Fear* (1943) were complex stories marred by a combination of tight budgets and studio re-editing. *The Lady from Shanghai* (1948), despite moments of brilliance, puzzled viewers with its baffling narrative and appalled Hollywood by casting Rita Hayworth as a murderess. Three efforts to film Shakespeare—*Macbeth* (1948), *Othello* (1952), and *Chimes at Midnight* (1966: an ingenious dramatic brew drawn from five plays and centering on the figure of Falstaff)—did little to boost his popular appeal. When

Welles did manage to bring a project in on time and on budget, as he did with *The Stranger* (1946), he considered his work artistically inferior. For all his dramatic energy and technical virtuosity, nearly all his films were commercial flops. His film career is a classic case of an individual auteur at odds with the studio system.

Welles spent ten years in Europe, where the climate was more favorable to auteurs, and on returning to the United States took on acting and television jobs to help finance his films. In his later years, Hollywood gave him numerous awards, but most of his film ideas were never realized. The promise of a legendary life, as one critic observed, became a lifeless legend, not unlike the plight of Charles Foster Kane (McBride 1977, 7).

Anyone searching for technical originality will find examples in abundance in *Citizen Kane*. Look for the sequence that compresses an entire marriage into a swift montage of breakfast-table scenes. Or the heady low-angle shots of Kane looming above the people he desires to master. Or the low-key lighting in the death and the newsroom scenes, where obscurity is both literal and figurative. Or the overlapping sounds when Kane's applause for Susan dissolves into applause for his own political campaign. Or the long crane shots that lift us to the rooftop of the El Rancho nightclub, through the rain-pocked skylight, then down to the single table where Susan sits alone. Or the sepulchral rooms in Xanadu, where an aged Kane is dwarfed by his own fireplace, sixteen feet high and ten feet deep.

Beyond its structural innovations and cinematic virtuosity, *Citizen Kane* is a compelling study of character. Kane is different things to different people: idealist and materialist, Communist and Fascist, philanthropist and egotist. His climb to wealth and power traces one version of the American Dream (the film's working title was *The American*), yet the film also shows Kane's tragic decline to impotent solitude. Bernstein describes him as "a man who got everything he wanted and then lost it." For all his material gifts to Susan, she accuses Kane of being fundamentally selfish: "You never really gave me anything that belongs to you, that you care about." Leland has his own explanation: "I guess all he wanted out of life was love . . . he just didn't have any to give."

Kane's need for love is suggested early in the film, during the Colorado scene when he is taken from his mother as a child. The themes of lost childhood and unreciprocated love are reinforced by the "Rosebud" motif in Herrmann's score, and culminates in the final views of Kane's enormous mansion, his monument and mausoleum, filled with a lifetime of accumulated objects. The moving camera hovers over all these things, then stops to focus on a single item being cast into the furnace. Is this the answer to the film's main question, or a hoax, or just another piece of life's unsolvable puzzle?

Suggested Films and Readings

More Films by Orson Welles

> *The Magnificent Ambersons* (1942)
>
> *The Stranger* (1946)
>
> *The Lady from Shanghai* (1948)
>
> *Macbeth* (1948)
>
> *Othello* (1952)
>
> *Mr. Arkadin* (1955)
>
> *Touch of Evil* (1958)
>
> *The Trial* (1962)
>
> *Chimes at Midnight* (1966)
>
> *The Immortal Story* (1968)

Books about Orson Welles and Citizen Kane

Carringer, Robert L. 1985. *The Making of* Citizen Kane. Berkeley: University of California Press.

> Carringer presents a case for studying *Citizen Kane* as a collaborative effort. His careful scholarship reveals a wealth of new material on every phase of filmmaking, including scripting, art direction, cinematography, postproduction, and release.

Cowie, Peter. 1973. *A Ribbon of Dreams: The Cinema of Orson Welles.* New York: A. S. Barnes.

> Cowie takes issue with Pauline Kael's claims that Mankiewicz should be given credit for much of the script. His portrait of Welles takes in the whole sweep of his career as a director, actor, and professional personality.

Gottesman, Ronald, ed. 1976. *Focus on Orson Welles.* Englewood Cliffs, N.J.: Prentice-Hall.

> This useful collection of contemporary reviews, documents, and criticism includes articles by Peter Bogdanovich and David Bordwell.

Kael, Pauline. 1971. *The* Citizen Kane *Book.* Boston: Little, Brown.

Kael's famous article claiming that Mankiewicz really wrote the script is reprinted together with the shooting script and cutting continuity.

McBride, Joseph. 1977. *Orson Welles, Actor and Director.* New York: Harvest/HBJ Books.

Focusing on politics and psychology, McBride places *Citizen Kane* in the context of cultural history.

Naremore, James. 1978. *The Magic World of Orson Welles.* New York: Oxford University Press.

This is the first full academic treatment of Welles.

Taylor, John Russell. 1986. *Orson Welles: A Celebration.* Boston: Little, Brown.

Taylor's book is a lively pictorial celebration of the man and his work.

Questions for Reflection and Discussion

1. *Citizen Kane* is a story told from differing points of view. We learn about Charles Foster Kane from a newsreel, from interviews with people who knew him, and from a restlessly inquiring camera. Discuss the use of multiple perspectives in the film. How well do these versions agree with one another? How complete is the final picture they present of Kane?

2. Consider Kane's motivations and conflicts in the film. What does he want from the newspaper business? From politics? From Susan Alexander? From life? What stands in his way? How successful is he in the end?

3. Kane is a man who builds monuments: Xanadu, the opera house, a newspaper empire. What drives him to build these things? What kind of satisfaction do they bring him?

4. Much attention is given to the word "Rosebud" in *Citizen Kane.* Explain what you think it means, and tell how important it is to our final understanding of Charles Foster Kane.

5. *Citizen Kane* was applauded for its innovative uses of sound, such as overlapping sound montage. Describe how the film uses sound to tell the story and contribute to the themes.

6. Orson Welles uses the medium of film to comment on the media of print journalism, radio, and film itself. Cite examples from

Citizen Kane to show what you believe Welles wants us to think about these media.

7. *Citizen Kane* is known for its creative use of deep-focus photography and low-key lighting. Describe the ways these techniques contribute to the atmosphere and the meaning of the film.

8. At the end of his life, Kane's mansion is filled with things he has collected. Not only does he collect objects, but he tries to collect people as well. How do you account for this? What does Kane's urge for collecting reveal about his character?

9. In one scene, Kane opens an envelope from Leland and finds his check for $25,000 torn to pieces. Also in the envelope is a Declaration of Principles from earlier years. Kane rips up the declaration as Susan looks on. Trace the relationship of Kane and Leland up to this point. What do the torn documents—the check and the declaration—tell about their friendship and conflicts?

10. Near the end of his newspaper investigation, Thompson sums up Kane's life and adds, "All the same, I can't help feeling sorry for him." Give your own evaluation of Charles Foster Kane, the public figure and the private person. Do you feel that sympathy or pity is justified? Explain.

Topics for Further Study

1. Read about the controversy over who should receive credit for *Citizen Kane*. Begin with Pauline Kael's claims in *The Citizen Kane Book* that Mankiewicz, not Welles, was chiefly responsible for the idea and the script. Next read the replies by Peter Bogdanovich (in Gottesman's *Focus on Orson Welles*) and Peter Cowie (*A Ribbon of Dreams*). Then decide if Robert Carringer's study, *The Making of Citizen Kane*, represents the final word.

2. Find out more about William Randolph Hearst, the newspaper monopolist who believed that Charles Foster Kane was a deliberate caricature of himself. Was Hearst justified in his belief? Was he justified in taking measures to halt the film's distribution?

3. Take a closer look at some key scenes from the film. Here are some suggestions:

   • The framing of the characters in the Colorado scene and in Susan's apartment after Kane's campaign speech.

- The lighting in the opening scene (Kane's death), the newsreel screening room, and the birthday party scene.
- The camera angles in key encounters: Kane and Leland in the newspaper office after his campaign defeat, Kane and Susan in their apartment after Leland is fired.
- The set design in the *Inquirer* office and in Xanadu.
- The use of montage in the breakfast-table sequence.
- The deep-focus photography in Susan's bedroom, after the overdose of sleeping pills.
- The camera movement in the El Rancho scenes and in the interior shots of Kane's mansion.
- The sound transitions in the sequence beginning with Susan playing the piano and singing and ending with Kane's campaign speech, or between Christmas and New Year's at the Thatcher residence.
- Bernard Herrmann's "power" and "Rosebud" musical motifs at the beginning and ending of the film.
- Two views of the same event: Susan's opera debut in Chicago.

8 On the Waterfront

Directed by Elia Kazan; produced by Sam Spiegel; script by Budd Schulberg; based on newspaper articles by Malcolm Johnson; photography by Boris Kaufman; edited by Gene Milford; art direction by Richard Day; music by Leonard Bernstein; released by Columbia in 1954. [108 minutes]

Terry Malloy . . . . *Marlon Brando*
Edie Doyle . . . . *Eva Marie Saint*
Father Barry . . . . *Karl Malden*
Johnny Friendly . . . . *Lee J. Cobb*
Charley Malloy . . . . *Rod Steiger*
"Kayo" Dugan . . . . *Pat Henning*

Elia Kazan (pronounced Ee-LI-a KAY-zan) was born in 1909 to a Greek family in Turkey and immigrated to New York at the age of four. His father became a rug merchant, successful enough to send his son to Williams College. Bright, ambitious, and intense, Kazan went on to study drama at Yale and joined the radical Group Theater in 1932. Later, the director would remember his feelings of estrangement during those years—a Greek in Anatolia, an immigrant at Williams—an estrangement which led him to join the Communist Party. "I was ready then to play the leading role in *Waiting for Lefty*. I was full of anger, silent, unexpressed anger" (Ciment 1974, 13). In the Group Theater, Kazan met Lee Strasberg and Harold Clurman, American exponents of the Stanislavsky method of acting, which had such a profound influence on his own directing style. Kazan worked on plays, as assistant stage manager and playwright, but he also became fascinated by the power of films. In college, he had been struck by Eisenstein's *Potemkin* (1925). Now he worked on documentary films with Ralph Steiner, Leo Hurwitz, and Paul Strand. In his plays and films, the messages were intensely political. "I was trying to say, 'There is a social conflict going on that influences and determines individual behavior'" (Ciment 1974, 16).

In the 1940s Kazan gained a reputation directing Broadway plays by Thornton Wilder, Tennessee Williams, and Arthur Miller. In the

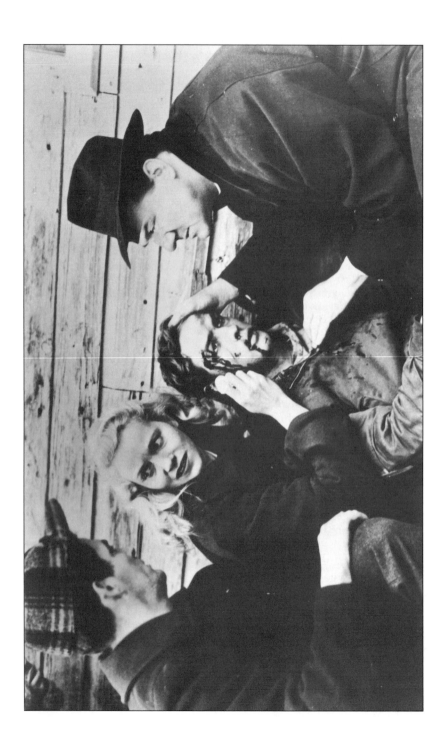

mid-forties, he began directing feature films. His films took on strong themes. *Gentleman's Agreement* (1947) was an indictment of anti-Semitism. *Pinky* (1949) was an early attack on racism. *Viva Zapata!* (1952) championed the Mexican revolutionary hero, Emiliano Zapata.

The genesis of *On the Waterfront* (1954) is no less dramatic than the film itself. Arthur Miller had originally worked on a waterfront script, which he called *The Hook,* a reference to the Red Hook section of Brooklyn and a tool, resembling the Communist sickle, used by longshoremen. Miller abandoned the script during the anti-Communist fervor preceding the rise of Senator Joseph McCarthy. Then, in 1952, Kazan was called to testify before the House Un-American Activities Committee (HUAC). First secretly, then in open hearings, Kazan admitted his party membership, renouncing his past affiliations and naming other "sympathizers." Arthur Miller was among those named. Miller responded with his play, *The Crucible* (1953), which represented the McCarthy hearings as a Salem witch-hunt. For his part, Kazan was allowed to continue at Twentieth Century-Fox, and *On the Waterfront* can be seen as an act of self-justification. Like Kazan, Terry Malloy testifies against a group to which he once belonged. "Terry felt as I did," Kazan once explained. "He felt ashamed and proud of himself at the same time" (Ciment 1974, 110).

For the screenplay, Kazan called in the writer Budd Schulberg. Together they visited the docks around Manhattan and learned first-hand about the mob. Schulberg recalls, "At least ten percent of everything that moved in and out of the harbor went into the pockets of these desperados. And if you were one of the 25,000 longshoremen looking for work, either you kicked back to a hiring boss appointed by mob overlords . . . or they starved you off the docks" (Schulberg 1980, 142–43).

Some of the characters in Schulberg's script are based on real people. Father Barry (played by Karl Malden) was inspired by Father John Corridan, "a tall, fast-talking, chain-smoking, hardheaded, sometimes profane Kerryman" known as "the waterfront priest" (Schulberg 1980, 143). Kayo Dugan (Pat Henning) was based on Arthur Browne, a feisty disciple of Father John who introduced the writer to the back streets. Much of Schulberg's research is documented in *Waterfront* (1955), the novel which he published one year after the film's release.

One hallmark of the film is its location. *On the Waterfront* was Kazan's first film to be made in New York, partly as a statement against Hollywood's climate of fantasy. In New York, Kazan pointed out, there is always "contact with reality" (Ciment 1974, 105). In fact, the contact was so real that longshoremen had to protect the film crew from the waterfront mob. Kazan was conscious of working within the genre of the gangster movie; he wanted to use it as a way to tell the story of the working class. The genre, he said, was "a breakthrough into working-class life . . . the first view from underneath" (Ciment 1974, 105). It was also among the first cinematic forays into the realism of on-location photography. The realistic texture of this film is reflected in Boris Kaufman's gritty black-and-white photography, his naturalistic lighting, the lack of distracting editing or camera movement, and the use of ambient sounds: the foghorns, pile drivers, and whistles that keep obscuring—and heightening—the dialogue.

Another hallmark is the film's realistic performances, particularly that of Marlon Brando. Kazan considered Brando a genius among actors: "You put things in him and then you wait, as if it's going to hibernate or something; and then it comes out later" (Ciment 1974, 106). For Kazan, Brando represented method acting at its best. Brando internalized his role, absorbing the character of Terry Malloy so that his speech and gestures were intuitively right. The scene where Terry walks Edie (Eva Marie Saint) home is a good example. During the shooting, Eva accidentally dropped her glove. Brando picked it up and held it as a way of holding her, then put his hand inside it, expressing an intimacy that Terry wanted but could not express in words (Ciment 1974, 45–46). As a disciple of the Stanislavski acting method, Kazan always stressed what each character wanted in a scene: "What are you on stage *for*? What do you walk on stage to get?" (Ciment 1974, 41). He also emphasized what happened just before the scene, where the character has come from. This gives strong motivation and continuity to action on the screen. It transfers the burden of meaning from what is said to how it is said, from dialogue to facial movements, gestures, and objects. That is why so many of the words in *On the Waterfront* are eclipsed by other things, and why the obstruction doesn't matter.

The movie was a great success. It grossed more than $4 million, and it won no fewer than nine academy awards, including two for Kazan (best film, best director), two for Schulberg (best story, best screenplay), and one each for Brando (best actor), Eva Marie Saint (best supporting actress), Boris Kaufman (best cinematography), Richard Day (best art direction), and Gene Milford (best editing). Though the critical reception was mixed, partly due to Kazan's appearance before HUAC, the film remains among his finest work for the screen.

Suggested Films and Readings

More Films by Elia Kazan

    A Tree Grows in Brooklyn (1945)

    Boomerang (1947)

    Gentleman's Agreement (1947)

    Pinky (1949)

    A Streetcar Named Desire (1951)

    Viva Zapata! (1952)

    East of Eden (1955)

    Baby Doll (1956)

    A Face in the Crowd (1957)

    Splendor in the Grass (1961)

    America, America (1963)

    The Arrangement (1969)

    The Visitors (1972)

Books about Elia Kazan, Marlon Brando, and On the Waterfront

Carey, Gary. 1985. *Marlon Brando: The Only Contender.* New York: St. Martin's Press.

A lucid, informed account of Brando's private and professional life by a writer steeped in movie lore.

Ciment, Michel. 1974. *Kazan on Kazan.* New York: Viking.

This sequence of interviews covers Kazan's life from his birth in Turkey to his 1970s films. It offers an inside view of the philosophy and personality behind the screen.

Kazan, Elia. 1988. *Elia Kazan: A Life. New York: Knopf.*

Pauly, Thomas H. 1983. *An American Odyssey: Elia Kazan and American Culture.* Philadelphia: Temple University Press.

Schulberg, Budd. 1980. On the Waterfront: *The Final Shooting Script.* Hollywood: Samuel French.

Includes the original screenplay and an informative afterword by the script writer.

————. 1955. *Waterfront*. New York: Random House.

Schulberg wrote this novel a year after the film, changing the ending and filling in the results of his research into union racketeering on the New York docks.

Thomas, Tony. 1973. *The Films of Marlon Brando*. Secaucus, N.J.: Citadel Press.

This film-by-film synopsis of the actor's work for the screen contains useful background information about each film.

Questions for Reflection and Discussion

1. Terry Malloy becomes a witness against his former friends. In some circumstances, such a person might be called a "whistle-blower" or a "stool pigeon"; yet most viewers see Terry as a hero. How would you describe him? Where do you draw the line between group loyalty and social responsibility?

2. Early in the film, Terry describes his philosophy of life to Edie: "Do it to him before he does it to you." Where else does he articulate the code he lives by? At what point does he begin to question it? Why?

3. *On the Waterfront* is also a love story. Trace the relationship between Terry and Edie. What do they see in each other? What do they give to one another? What are they left with at the end?

4. Kazan made *On the Waterfront* in New York, not Hollywood, because he wanted "contact with reality." How successful was he in capturing the authentic feel of life on the docks? What contributes to the film's realism? Consider the locations, camera work, dialogue, and style of acting.

5. Marlon Brando won an Oscar for his role as Terry Malloy. Many critics still consider it his best performance, despite a long, successful career of acting, which includes the roles of Stanley Kowalski in *A Streetcar Named Desire* (1951) and Don Corleone in *The Godfather* (1972). Comment on Brando's strengths and limitations as an actor. What kinds of roles does he seem best suited for? What personal qualities and techniques work for him when he's at his best?

6. While *On the Waterfront* is widely noted for its realistic qualities, there are symbolic touches throughout the film. Consider the pigeons, the stevedores' hooks, the platform on which Father

Barry rises with Kayo's body from the hold. What might these things represent? Do their symbolic functions detract from the film's realism, or do they add something important?

7. The film's music was scored by Leonard Bernstein, who later did the sound for *West Side Story* (1961). What similarities do you hear between the sound tracks of these films? How does Bernstein use jazz sounds and the syncopated rhythms of the docks to create a mood for the story?

8. The last words of the movie are Johnny Friendly's: "I'll be back." What do you think he means? Considering his threat, how optimistic is the ending?

Topics for Further Study

1. Elia Kazan made *On the Waterfront* two years after he testified before HUAC, the House Un-American Activities Committee. A former member of the Communist Party, Kazan publicly renounced all party affiliations and gave the names of former friends who had been party members. Some who saw the film in 1954 drew parallels between Kazan and Terry Malloy. Find out more about the HUAC hearings and Kazan's conduct as a witness. You may want to compare *On the Waterfront* with two plays by Arthur Miller, *The Crucible* (1953) and *A View from the Bridge* (1955), both of which deal with the issue of testifying from a very different point of view.

2. Think of other films in which the hero testifies against his peers. In *Serpico* (1973), an honest cop (played by Al Pacino) tries to expose corruption among his fellow police officers. In *Casualties of War* (1989), an army private named Erikson (Michael J. Fox) exposes four war buddies who raped and killed a young woman in Vietnam. Like Terry Malloy, Serpico and Private Erikson face tremendous pressures from a corrupt establishment, whether it be the mob, the police force, or the army. What drives them to struggle against such overwhelming odds? Do you consider them courageous, foolhardy, stubborn, or something else?

3. In his 1955 novel, *Waterfront*, Budd Schulberg writes about the millions of dollars siphoned from legitimate trade by the mob that rules the docks. "Just tack it onto the cost, it's part of the business, all part of the game. Nobody really feels it except the consumer, you'n'me, and we're too dumb to complain." How do you respond to Schulberg's remarks?

4. In his afterword to the published shooting script (1980, 151–52), Schulberg tells how the producer, Sam Spiegel, thought Father Barry's speech about Kayo Dugan's death (pp. 78–83 in the script) was much too long for a movie. Schulberg defended the length of this "Sermon on the Docks," claiming it was true-to-life and essential to the theme. Review the scene. Do you agree with Spiegel or Schulberg? What film techniques did Kazan use to make the scene more cinematic?

5. Analyze these other scenes:

   • Terry picks up Edie's glove while walking her home.

   • Terry confesses to Father Barry and Edie against a background of smoke, whistles, and pile drivers.

   • Terry says to his brother in the car, "I could have been a contender."

   • Compare the two scenes of Terry and Jimmy at the rooftop pigeon coop: "They got it made." "A pigeon for a pigeon."

   • Compare the crowd scenes: the dock workers scrambling for work tabs; cowering back when Terry fights Johnny Friendly; falling in behind Terry in the final scene.

9 Rebel Without a Cause

Directed by Nicholas Ray; produced by David Weisbart; screenplay by Stewart Stern; based on an adaptation by Irving Schulman of a story idea by Nicholas Ray; title from a book by Dr. Robert Lindner (1944); cinematography by Ernest Haller; set decoration by William Wallace; music by Leonard Rosenman; edited by William Ziegler; released by Warners in 1955. [111 minutes]

Jim Stark	James Dean
Judy	Natalie Wood
Plato	Sal Mineo
Ray Stark	Jim Backus
Mrs. Stark	Ann Doran
Buzz Gunderson	Corey Allen
Goon	Dennis Hopper
Crunch	Frank Mazzola
Judy's Father	William Hopper

In the mid-1950s, rebellious youth were running rampant on the screen. Brando had terrorized small-town America with his motorcycle gang in *The Wild One* (1954). Sidney Poitier had played one of the troubled city high school students in *The Blackboard Jungle* (1955). Such was the climate when Nicholas Ray cast James Dean in the title role of *Rebel Without a Cause*. Ray took his title from a book published by Robert Lindner in 1944, the story of an imprisoned juvenile delinquent who could give no reasons for his crimes. As a sociologist, Lindner had studied the postwar generation of youth—often violent and inarticulate—which he believed was rebelling against conformity. Ray was intrigued by Lindner's views; he talked to law officers and young offenders, then wrote a short synopsis for the film. He created the roles of Jim and Judy with *Romeo and Juliet* in mind because he considered Shakespeare's play "the best play about juvenile delinquents" (Kreidl 1977, 79).

The evolution of the script is a good example of how a film idea passes through many hands. Leon Uris, the author of *Exodus* (1957), tried to make it a story about communal action. Irving Schulman

transferred the setting from a Polish urban neighborhood to middle-class California, then added the planetarium sequence and the "chickie run," (drag racing to the edge of a cliff, the first driver bailing out being "chicken") which he had read about in a newspaper. When Stewart Stern received the script, he reshaped it along Freudian lines, drawing on his own father for the character Ray Stark. All along, Nicholas Ray collaborated on the writing. For him, the central focus was "the problem of the individual's desire to preserve himself in the face of overwhelming demands for social conformism" (Kreidl 1977, 88).

Nicholas Ray (1911–79) was born Raymond Nicholas Kienzle in LaCrosse, Wisconsin. He had studied architecture under Frank Lloyd Wright, then tried acting in the Group Theater under Elia Kazan and in the Phoenix Theater under John Houseman. In 1944, he assisted Kazan on the set of *A Tree Grows in Brooklyn*. From 1949 to 1963, Ray directed more than sixteen films, specializing in Hollywood genres like Westerns, war films, and film noir. They all bear his personal stamp: the kinetic movements of his camera, a keen eye for color, the emphasis on social forces, and lone heroes in search of an authentic life. Andrew Sarris saw Ray's films as "the indisputable record of a very personal anguish," one that summed up "all the psychic ills of the fifties" (1968, 108–109). If you want a glimpse of this director, look for him as the man with a briefcase walking toward the planetarium in the final shot of *Rebel Without a Cause*.

If Nicholas Ray became a kind of cult hero among film critics and directors, James Dean (1931–55) became an even greater idol among young viewers. When Dean was killed in an auto accident at the age of twenty-four, he left a legacy of only three feature films. For two of his performances, both directed by Elia Kazan (*East of Eden*, 1955; *Giant*, 1956), he had won Academy Awards for best actor. Like Brando, Dean was a disciple of the Stanislavsky method. François Truffaut described Dean's acting as "more animal than human," noting how "he acts beyond what he is saying; he plays alongside the scene" (1976, 297). Yet off the set, Dean could be articulate about his philosophy of performance: "In the short span of his lifetime an actor must learn all there is to know, experience all there is to experience, or approach that state as closely as possible. . . . To grasp the full significance of life is the actor's duty; to interpret it his problem; and to express it his dedication" (Howlett 1975, Dedication).

From the first shot of the film, Dean's talent is at work. While the credits roll, we see him playing on the sidewalk with a windup toy monkey. It is a whimsical moment—the youth is a bit tipsy—but it reveals the sensitive child within. On the sound track, a dissonant jazz piece mingles with the strident scream of sirens. Amid the sounds of discord is a cry for help. In the police station, Jim mimics the sirens. His tie and jacket barely cover his emotional dishevelment. In another room, Judy is being questioned about her father. "He called me a dirty tramp," she says, a reproach reflected in her red lipstick and red coat. In yet another room, a sullen, clean-cut boy cannot explain why he has drowned a litter of puppies. This is Plato, left by his parents in a housekeeper's care. "Nobody can help me," he says. These three teenagers in trouble will soon be linked. For now, their common cause is represented by the setting and highlighted by the camera, which isolates their faces through selective framing and oblique angles.

Later in the film, the context widens. We are introduced to the families, and we see their large, suburban homes. In the planetarium, the context becomes cosmic. "The problems of man seem trivial indeed," intones the professor of astronomy, while a cataclysmic ending of the earth is enacted on the dome overhead—a movie in a movie. Plato whispers, "What does he know about man alone?" Back on earth, the issues acquire Freudian overtones. Jim's father, wearing an apron, appears weak and foolish; he fails to be the male authority his son is yearning for. Judy's father won't respond to her affection; he would rather tousle his son's hair than accept his daughter's kiss. Plato's housekeeper is sympathetic, but no substitute for a real parent. So these teenagers adrift are left to work out their inner tumult in knife games, gangs, and chickie fights. They rebel with reasons, but without a cause.

Suggested Films and Readings

More Films by Nicholas Ray

> *They Live by Night* (1947)
>
> *Knock on Any Door* (1949)
>
> *Born to Be Bad* (1950)
>
> *In a Lonely Place* (1950)
>
> *Flying Leathernecks* (1951)
>
> *Johnny Guitar* (1954)
>
> *The True Story of Jesse James* (1957)

Books about Rebel, Nicholas Ray, *and* James Dean

Bast, William. 1956. *James Dean: A Biography.* New York: Ballantine.

Howlett, John. 1975. *James Dean: A Biography.* New York: Simon & Schuster.

Kreidl, John Francis. 1977. *Nicholas Ray.* Boston: Twayne.

More than one hundred pages are devoted to *Rebel Without a Cause*: its 1950s background, development from scenario to film, close analyses of key scenes, and international reception.

Morella, Joe, and Edward Z. Epstein. 1971. *Rebels: The Rebel Hero in Films.* New York: Citadel.

In a compelling narrative and abundant photographs, this book traces the image of rebellious youth in American cinema from John Garfield and the Dead End Kids to Marlon Brando, James Dean, Peter Fonda, and a gallery of other cinematic anti-heroes.

Sarris, Andrew. 1968. *The American Cinema: Directors and Directions, 1929–1968.* New York: Dutton.

Contains a brief, insightful summary of Ray's achievements.

Stern, Stewart. 1986. *Rebel Without a Cause.* In Sam Thomas, ed., *Best American Screenplays.* New York: Crown Publishers.

Stern's screenplay for the movie is reprinted in this useful anthology.

Truffaut, François. 1978. "James Dean Is Dead." In Leonard Mayhew, tr., *The Films in My Life.* New York: Simon & Schuster.

A tribute to the actor by one of his most famous European admirers.

Questions for Reflection and Discussion

1. *Rebel Without a Cause* is sometimes seen as the classic study of youth rebelling against conformity. Considering the pressures of family, community, and peer groups in this film, does the rebel have a cause?

2. Jim, Judy, and Plato are introduced in the first police-station sequence. What do we learn about their background from this sequence? How are their problems connected? Why are their lives about to be linked?

3. Nicholas Ray is known for the deliberate imbalance of his camera work and his unusual way of cutting between shots. Select an

action scene from the movie (the knife fight, the chickie run, the attack on Plato in the mansion) and analyze the film techniques which make the scene effective. Consider the elements of music and lighting as well.

4. The filming of this movie was originally conceived in black and white, but Ray turned to color soon after shooting began. Note the color of Jim's jacket, Judy's coat, Plato's socks, and other items in the film. What kinds of statements about character and setting are made through color?

5. Nicholas Ray has explained that one intention in *Rebel Without a Cause* was to revive the story of *Romeo and Juliet*, which he considered to be the best play about juvenile delinquents. In what ways are Jim and Judy like Romeo and Juliet? What difference does the shift in setting make from Renaissance Italy to modern California? You may want to compare Ray's film with a later film version of *Romeo and Juliet: West Side Story* (1961).

6. Several key scenes occur at or in the Griffith Planetarium. What makes this an effective setting? How does the planetarium gain symbolic meanings as the film progresses?

7. The word "chicken" is a recurring motif in the film. Why is it such an important word for Jim? What does it represent in Jim's perception of himself, his family, and his peers?

8. Before the chickie run, Jim turns to Buzz and asks, "Why do we do this?" Buzz replies, "We have to do something." What insights does the film offer into the nature of youth gangs and their alternatives?

9. Jim is a newcomer to the neighborhood and an outsider at Dawson High. How is his estrangement shown in the film? In what other ways is he an outsider? Does he find a place where he belongs?

10. Compare *Rebel Without a Cause* and *On the Waterfront*. Consider the characters of Jim Stark and Terry Malloy—young men in trouble; Plato and Jimmy—boys who look to them as older brothers; Judy and Edie—the young women in their lives; and Ray, the juvenile officer, and Father Barry—the father figures.

Topics for Further Study

1. The release of *Rebel Without a Cause* coincided with other films about juvenile delinquency, notably *The Wild Ones* and *Blackboard*

Jungle. Compare the settings, characters, and themes of these three films. What do they communicate about youth and rebellion in the 1950s? How do they compare with later movies on the subject?

2. In his book, *Nicholas Ray*, John Kreidl traces the development of *Rebel Without a Cause* from its genesis in Dr. Lindner's study of a juvenile offender to the final shooting script. Read this or other accounts of the film's origins, and learn how each individual (script writers, director, musical director, actors) contributed to the production. To what extent is this film the personal vision of the director or a collaborative effort?

3. James Dean died in an auto accident soon after this film was made. His death, and his performance in two other movies (*East of Eden* and *Giant*), made him a cult figure for his generation. Read more about his life, and explain why you think he was so important in his time. Who, if anyone, corresponds to James Dean in our own time?

4. The opening scene shows Jim Stark playing with a windup monkey on the street, while the dissonant sounds of jazz and police sirens fill the sound track. There are many such moments in the film, when sounds and images carry more meaning than words. Select a few such moments and explain why you think they are important.

5. More scenes to analyze:

- The breakfast scenes in the homes of Jim and Judy.

- The editing of action in the knife game outside the planetarium, the chickie fight on the cliff, and the attack on Plato in the mansion.

- The camera angles in the scene when Jim tells his father about the Buzz's death.

- The use of lighting in the planetarium scenes.

10 The Graduate

Directed by Mike Nichols; produced by Lawrence Turman; screenplay by Calder Willingham and Buck Henry, based on the novel by Charles Webb; photography by Robert Surtees; edited by Sam O'Steen; production design by Richard Sylbert; set decoration by George Nelson; songs by Paul Simon, sung by Simon and Garfunkel; additional music by Dave Grusin; released by Embassy Pictures in 1967. [105 minutes]

Mrs. Robinson	*Anne Bancroft*
Benjamin Braddock	*Dustin Hoffman*
Elaine Robinson	*Katharine Ross*
Mr. Braddock	*William Daniels*
Mrs. Braddock	*Elizabeth Wilson*
Room Clerk	*Buck Henry*
Carl Smith	*Brian Avery*
Mr. McGuire	*Walter Brooke*
Mr. McCleery	*Norman Fell*

The Graduate spans two settings, two cultures, two generations, two women, and two genres. It tells the story of a young man, home from college, who confronts the sounds of silence in the house where he was raised. A successful student by his parents' yardstick, he has not yet measured up to his own standards, nor does he know yet what those standards are. Seduced by the neighbor's wife, he finds himself morally and emotionally adrift, until the neighbor's daughter gives him something to live for. When Ben abandons Mrs. Robinson for Elaine, he forsakes the empty surburban lifestyle of Los Angeles for a more authentic alternative in Berkeley. With this shift, the film modulates from satire to romance, but it never leaves the key of solitude.

The Graduate enjoyed immense critical and popular acclaim when it appeared in 1967. Mike Nichols won an Academy Award for his directing; Dustin Hoffman, Anne Bancroft, and Katharine Ross received acting nominations; Simon and Garfunkel won a Grammy Award for their music sound track; Calder Willingham and Buck Henry received a Writer's Guild award for their script. The film itself won the Golden Globe and the British Film Academy awards. After more than a decade of declining film attendance and artistic reputation, here was a break-through in American cinema. Stanley Kauffmann thought that Nichols's achievement gave viewers reason to believe that American films were coming of age. He called the film "a milestone in American film history" (1971, 41); Warren French called it "the picture of its generation" (Schuth 1978, Editor's Foreword).

Not everyone agreed. Pauline Kael regarded *The Graduate* as an "aesthetically trivial movie" that "domesticates alienation for the masses" (1970, 127). Andrew Sarris took Nichols to task for following the commercial mainstream, dubbing his work "the cinema and theater of complicity." Sarris warned that "the customer is always right except in the long view of eternity" (1968, 218).

While the long view may not yet be available, Nichols's career has continued for another two successful decades. Born in a Jewish family in Berlin in 1931, Nichols came to the United States at the age of nine. After a brief study of medicine, he went into acting. In 1954, he started a life-long professional partnership with Elaine May, first as a comic radio team, then taking their social satire on the road to Broadway and beyond. A student of Lee Strasberg, he began directing plays in 1963 and films in 1966.

Nichols's directing style is stamped on every shot of *The Graduate*. It opens with a close-up of Dustin Hoffman's impassive face. The camera pulls back to reveal the interior of an airplane. We hear a disembodied voice announcing the descent into Los Angeles. As Hoffman moves mutely through the terminal, the sound track carries Simon and Garfunkel's song, "The Sound of Silence." In a medium shot, his luggage moves forward on a conveyor belt. A recorded voice drones on in the background. Mechanized motion, mechanized sound. More close-ups follow Hoffman as he retrieves his luggage and then disappears into the crowd. The scene dissolves to a close-up of his face, half in shadow, still impassive, viewed against the fish tank in his bedroom.

Benjamin Braddock, the college graduate, is home from school. Where Charles Webb's novel provides a narrative commentary on his alienation, the film gives us Hoffman's inert, isolated face to read. The camera isolates him as he weaves through crowds or idles in a pool. It frames his image behind the glass wall of a fishbowl or a telephone booth, reflects it in the backyard pool or a glass tabletop. When Ben appears at his birthday party in full scuba gear, we view the scene in a subjective shot from within his mask, the distorted faces of his parents and their guests mouthing words that neither he nor we can hear. This technique is repeated at the end of the film, when Ben raps on the plate-glass window of the church where Elaine's wedding is in progress; we see the angry gestures of the churchgoers from his point of view, without the sounds.

Nichols's camera comments on Ben's plight in other ways. When Ben races to the church, Nichols photographs the action head on, using a telephoto lens to emphasize the agonizing slowness of his progress. When Ben walks down the stairway to his graduation party, the camera pauses on a framed picture of an unhappy clown. Ben, too, is sadly on display, the "feature attraction" of the party. Elaine's portrait plays a similar role: In the bedroom scene when Elaine's mother asks Ben to unzip her dress, Mrs. Robinson moves out of frame, but the glass cover of the portrait reflects her nakedness. The daughter's innocent image is a mirror of the mother's sexual audacity.

The film's symbolism is sometimes subtle, sometimes heavy-handed. The fish tank in Ben's room contains a miniature diver. The backyard pool into which Ben plunges in his scuba outfit is the same pool on which he idly floats all summer long. The glass motif—repeated in the tabletop and phone booth, as well as in the windows of the car, the church, and the bus, is a variation on reflective surfaces that also isolate and obscure. Nichols also uses color to suggest qualities of character. Mrs. Robinson first appears in black, Elaine in pink. Ben's parents and their crowd are associated with blue and white, evoking coldness and sterility. In the later Berkeley scenes, Ben and Elaine are linked by warmer earth colors.

In his parents' milieu, where Ben was "just drifting," Nichols represents his disorientation in a montage of intermingled scenes. We see Ben emerge from his backyard pool, dry himself, and walk through a doorway. Now he is in the Taft Hotel with Mrs. Robinson. He lies in bed, rises, walks to the door, and emerges in his parents' kitchen. In the next shot he is back in bed, smoking a cigarette, watching the hotel television. A figure crosses the screen—it is Mrs. Robinson—and leaves the room. Now Ben gets out of bed and walks out—to the swimming pool. He dives in, then leaps onto the rubber raft . . . and into bed with Mrs. Robinson. As he turns toward the camera, we hear his father's voice saying, "What are you doing here?" A subjective shot shows Ben's parents peering down at him as he floats in the pool. The match-cuts between pool and bedroom illustrate Ben's confusion; the sound bridge—sound track preceding the image—intensifies it. Both techniques are persistent throughout the film.

Sound is a key element in this film about silences. Sometimes the discord accentuates the theme of alienation. In the drive-in scene, Ben and Elaine roll up the windows to isolate themselves from the surrounding din. In the scuba scene, Ben's heavy, rhythmic breathing contrasts with the partygoers' shallow chatter. Much of the film's thematic load is carried by Simon and Garfunkel, whose lyrics bridge the silences and tie the film together. "The Sound of Silence" describes the emptiness in Ben's surroundings: "People talking without speaking / People hearing without listening." "April Come She Will" plots the course of Ben's affair with Mrs. Robinson: "April, come she will . . . May, she will stay . . . June, she'll change her tune . . . August, die she must. . . ." "Scarborough Fair/Canticle," associated with Berkeley, anticipates a more promising relationship with Elaine. The songs of the sixties speak for those who cannot find the words.

Like Elia Kazan and Nicholas Ray, Mike Nichols followed Stanislavski's method of directing, which he learned from Lee Strasberg at the Actor's Studio in New York. The best performances in *The Graduate* appear natural, even understated, because the actors have internalized their roles. Katharine Ross as Elaine is genuinely sweet and innocent, dignified yet naive. Anne Bancroft's Mrs. Robinson is both manipulative and vulnerable. She seduces Ben with sophisticated poise, but when she turns her back to him in bed her face reveals her hidden pain. Dustin Hoffman plays the aimless graduate with understated conviction. In his solemn face, flat voice, and muffled whimper, we read the moral angst of a generation.

Nichols once described Ben as "a not particularly bright, not particularly remarkable, but worthy kid drowning among objects and things, committing moral suicide by allowing himself to be used" (Schuth 1978, 45). According to Nichols, "he doesn't have the moral or intellectual resources to do what a large percentage of other kids like him do—to rebel, to march, to demonstrate, to turn on. Just drowning" (Schuth 1978, 45).

Not all viewers agree. Stanley Kauffmann saw Ben as a "bright college graduate who . . . declines the options thrust upon him by barbecue-pit society." For Kauffmann, Ben is "a moralist—he wants to know the value of what he is doing" (1971, 37). Hollis Alpert concurred: "The most important thing in common between Elaine and Benjamin is that they share the urge to see honestly and clearly" (Schuth 1978, 61). The film contains what some might call "adult situations"—a seduction, bedroom scenes, a striptease act—but the point behind these moments is always an ethical one: young sensibilities calling adulthood to account. Perhaps that is why it is still popular with young audiences today.

Suggested Films and Readings

More Films by Mike Nichols

    Who's Afraid of Virginia Woolf? (1966)

    Catch-22 (1970)

    Carnal Knowledge (1971)

    The Day of the Dolphin (1973)

    The Fortune (1975)

    Regarding Henry (1991)

Books about Mike Nichols and The Graduate

Kael, Pauline. 1970. *Going Steady.* Boston: Little, Brown.

Kael's perceptive commentaries on contemporary films are available in this and other volumes of her collected criticism.

Gelmis, Joseph. 1970. *The Film Director as Superstar.* Garden City, N.Y.: Doubleday.

Includes an informative section on Nichols as film director.

Kauffmann, Stanley. 1971. "The Graduate." In *Figures of Light: Film Criticism and Comment.* New York: Harper & Row. 36–46.

Kauffmann's review, reprinted from the *The New York Times,* typifies the film's appreciative reception in 1967.

Samuels, Charles Thomas, ed. 1970. *A Casebook on Film.* New York: Van Nostrand Reinhold.

Features four essays on *The Graduate.*

Sarris, Andrew. !968. *The American Cinema: Directors and Directions, 1929–1968.* New York: Dutton.

A brief but influential appraisal of Nichols's place in the national cinema.

Schuth, H. Wayne. 1978. *Mike Nichols.* Boston: Twayne.

This first full-length book on Nichols dutifully traces his career in theater and film.

Webb, Charles. 1963. *The Graduate.* New York: Signet.

This is the bestselling novel on which Nichols based his film.

Willingham, Calder, and Buck Henry. 1986. "The Graduate." In Sam Thomas, ed., *Best American Screenplays*. New York: Crown.

The Willingham-Henry screenplay for the film.

Questions for Reflection and Discussion

1. The first image in *The Graduate* is a close-up of Ben's face. Then we see that he's alone on an airplane. How else does the film emphasize his solitude, his alienation from those around him? What accounts for his sense of isolation? Do you think he ever overcomes this feeling?

2. *The Graduate* was hailed in 1967 as *the* film of its generation. In what ways does it sum up the 1960s? In particular, how does it dramatize the "generation gap"?

3. Stanley Kauffmann, critic of *The New York Times*, praised *The Graduate* for its "moral stance." "Benjamin," he wrote, "is neither a laggard nor a lecher; he is, in the healthiest sense, a moralist— he wants to know the value of what he is doing." Consider Benjamin's moral dilemmas and behavior. What are his values, and how does he enact them?

4. Mrs. Robinson and her daughter, Elaine, are rivals for Ben's attention. How do you characterize them? What does each one see in Ben, and what does he see in them? What accounts for his movement from one to the other?

5. There are many images of water and glass throughout this film. Think of the swimming pool, the fishbowl in Ben's room, Ben's scuba mask, his sunglasses, and the many paintings, tabletops, and windows that reflect, reveal, or cover. Are they symbolic images? Are they merely part of Ben's visible world? How do they function in the film?

6. *The Graduate* is divided into two parts. There are two settings (Los Angeles and Berkeley), two generations and life-styles, two women, two sides of Benjamin, and perhaps two types of storytelling (satire and romance). Describe these contrasting aspects of the film. How are they related to each other and to the film's main themes?

7. Nichols is sometimes regarded as a "lightweight" director by the critics, although the films and plays that he directs are usually successful at the box office. How do you account for his popularity? Do you agree that he offers movies of artistic merit?

8. Viewers have noticed several film techniques that Nichols uses repeatedly in this film, including close-ups and overlapping sound transitions (in which the sound from a scene precedes its appearance on the screen). How innovative is the film from a technical point of view? How well does Nichols use standard film techniques?

9. Colors are associated with certain characters in *The Graduate.* Mrs. Robinson often wears black. Elaine appears in pink. The friends of Ben's parents are dressed in whites and blues. Trace the uses of color through the film. What is the effect of using colors in this way?

10. The final scene shows Ben and Elaine in the back of a departing bus. She is in her wedding gown. After catching their breath from their escape, they cease to look at one another as the sound track carries "The Sound of Silence." What do you think lies ahead for this couple?

Topics for Further Study

1. Nichols's film is based on the bestselling novel by Charles Webb. Scriptwriters Calder Willingham and Buck Henry adapted Webb's story for the screen, and Nichols made further changes on the set. Select a scene from the book and trace its evolution through the screenplay and the film. How do you account for the changes? How faithful is the filmed scene to the spirit of the original scene?

2. Much of the music in the film is taken from Simon and Garfunkel, including "The Sound of Silence," "Mrs. Robinson," "April Come She Will," "Scarborough Fair/Canticle," and "The Big Bright Green Pleasure Machine," all composed before *The Graduate* was made. Read the lyrics to these songs. How do they contribute to the film's moods and themes? How effectively do you think they are used?

3. More scenes to analyze:
   - Ben's arrival at the airport.
   - Ben's reception at his parents' home.
   - Ben at Mrs. Robinson's home.
   - Ben in scuba gear.

- Ben in the lobby of the Taft Hotel.
- Drifting montage: Ben floats between bed and pool.
- Ben and Elaine at the drive-in.
- Ben disrupts the wedding.

11 Mr. Smith Goes to Washington

Directed and produced by Frank Capra; screenplay by Sidney Buchman; based on Lewis R. Foster's story, "The Gentleman from Montana"; photography by Joseph Walker; art direction by Lionel Banks; music by Dimitri Tiomkin; editing by Gene Havlick and Al Clark; montage effects by Slavko Vorkapich; released by Columbia in 1939. [129 minutes]

Jefferson Smith	*James Stewart*
Clarissa Saunders	*Jean Arthur*
Senator Joseph Paine	*Claude Rains*
Jim Taylor	*Edward Arnold*
Governor Hubert	*Guy Kibbee*
Diz Moore	*Thomas Mitchell*
Chick McGann	*Eugene Pallette*
Ma Smith	*Beulah Bondi*
Senator Agnew	*H. B. Warner*
President of Senate	*Harry Carey*

The life story of Frank Capra (1897–1991) reads like a chapter from the American Dream. Born in Sicily at the end of last century, he was one of seven children in a family that could not read or write. After the Capras moved to California in 1903, he sold newspapers, played the banjo, and did other odd jobs to help out. By 1918, he had worked his way through UCLA, graduating with a degree in chemical engineering. After a brief stint in the army, he was unable to find work as an engineer. Instead, he found himself "hopping freights, selling photos house to house, hustling poker, playing guitars" (Capra 1971, 17). It was during these vagabond years that Capra learned about America firsthand, visiting the small towns and talking with the ordinary individuals who were to populate his films. "I got a real sense of small towns, got a real sense of America," he said to Richard Glatzer. "I met a lot of Gary Coopers" (1971, 31). As a door-to-door salesman, Capra sharpened his talent for telling—and selling— stories, another hallmark of his films. He was also learning to sell himself. In 1922, he convinced a small-time movie producer in San Francisco that

he was from Hollywood and thus made his first film. Within a few years, he had worked for Hal Roach, Mack Sennett, and Harry Langdon, among the best talent in the industry. In 1928, having learned the basics of his craft, Capra went to work for Harry Cohn at Columbia Pictures. This affiliation was to last for ten productive years.

Capra's films during these years reflect his populist vision of American ideals. In *Mr. Deeds Goes to Town* (1936), a tuba player from Mandrake Falls (Gary Cooper) inherits twenty million dollars and a Manhattan mansion but gives it all away to poor farmers in a Jeffersonian plan for redistributing wealth. In *Meet John Doe* (1941), a has-been baseball player (Cooper again) sets up John Doe clubs to empower common citizens against corrupt politicians. In *It's a Wonderful Life* (1946), the manager of a small-town Building and Loan company (James Stewart) struggles against a greedy banker and his own self-doubts to protect the good people of Bedford Falls.

In his heyday, Capra was immensely popular. Between 1932 and 1939, his films were nominated for Academy Awards in six out of seven years, and he won three times. He seemed, as Charles J. Maland believes, to have embodied the tensions and contradictions of American culture of that time (1980, 182). After World War II, however, Capra's views no longer squared with the changing political climate. He was accused of being a cinematic Norman Rockwell, a populist demagogue, a Fascist, a Socialist, and a purveyor of "Capra-corn." His reputation waned in the fifties and sixties, only to be restored in later years.

Mr. Smith Goes to Washington is based on a little-known story by Lewis Foster, "The Gentleman from Montana." Jefferson Smith is a patriotic American, one of the many decent people, as his name implies. Leader of the Boy Rangers, he is chosen by political boss James Taylor to replace the junior senator of his state when that senator dies. Taylor sees Smith as a puppet, but underestimates the depth of his convictions. When Smith introduces a bill to build a boy's camp on property that Taylor has been secretly acquiring, the political machine begins to roll against him. Smith puts up a heroic effort with the help of Clarissa Saunders, his secretary, but his cause is nearly crushed by the machine. Only the last-minute *crise de conscience* of senior senator Joseph Paine, who once championed "lost causes" with Smith's father, saves the day.

Capra was eager to make a film set in the nation's capital. In his autobiography, he describes how the crew went sightseeing through Washington on a bus, much like Mr. Smith; how he hired Jim Preston, superintendent of the Senate press gallery, to be his authenticity consultant; how a special introduction to the Press Club gave him material for the film; how all details of the Senate were studied and duplicated in the studio, down to the scar on Daniel Webster's desk (1971, 253–93). Authenticity was paramount. When Preston explained how the Senate clock was locked to keep senators from pushing the hands forward, Capra reproduced that detail on the set. Washington, D.C., seems more than a backdrop for the story; it is like a character whose presence is continuously felt. Slavko Vorkapich's montage of the Lincoln Memorial, Capitol Dome, and Union Station, and Dimitri Tiomkin's score of musical Americana ("Yankee Doodle," "My Country 'Tis of Thee," "Red River Valley," "When Johnny Comes Marching Home") contribute to this character and maintain the spirit of the film.

Capra used some unusual techniques to achieve the effects he wanted. When shooting close-ups, he played back tape-recorded sound tracks of the master shot to recapture the original tempo of the scene (Capra 1971, 275). To make James Stewart's voice hoarse during his twenty-four-hour filibuster, he had the actor's throat treated with mercury solution. Capra was involved in every phase of the production; even casting minor parts himself. "When interviewing, I didn't try to see the cast as actors," he recalls. "I tried to visualize them as human beings who were part of our story" (1971, 261). He haunted the editing room, cutting in reaction shots to comment on the action, like a Greek chorus (Glatzer 1975, 19). Even after the film was edited, his involvement did not stop. During previews, he taped the audience responses in order to have an objective record (Capra 1971, 278). This helped him gauge the impact of each scene.

Mr. Smith was ready only two months after World War II broke out in Europe. Because the film depicted political corruption at the highest levels, many were opposed to its release. Ambassador Joseph Kennedy feared it would destroy morale abroad. Other studios offered as much as two million dollars to keep it out of distribution. But Capra persevered. It became his most successful film financially, earning over five million dollars in domestic revenues (Maland 1980, 109). The key to that success may be found in the film's underlying attitude. As critics have pointed out, Capra offers no radical analysis of social and economic woes; rather, he calls for a return to traditional American values. He may distrust the leaders, but he has an abiding faith in the people themselves—and this, perhaps, is why people still watch his films.

Suggested Films and Readings

More Films by Frank Capra

   The Strong Man (1926)

   Platinum Blonde (1931)

It Happened One Night (1934)

Mr. Deeds Goes to Town (1936)

Lost Horizon (1937)

You Can't Take It with You (1938)

Meet John Doe (1941)

"Why We Fight" series (1942–1945)

Why We Fight: The Battle of Britain (1943)

It's a Wonderful Life (1946)

Books about Frank Capra

Capra, Frank. 1971. *The Name above the Title: An Autobiography.* New York: Macmillan.

Capra's lively autobiography offers an inside view of the personality and life experiences that shaped his films.

Carney, Raymond. 1986. *American Vision: The Films of Frank Capra.* New York: Cambridge University Press.

The most detailed study of Capra's life and work presents him as a visionary with affinities to the romantic and transcendental traditions of American literature.

Gallagher, Brian. 1986. "Using Film Segments to Teach Narrative-Descriptive Writing." *Teaching English in the Two-Year College.* Vol. 13: 273–80.

Gallagher describes a successful exercise in collaborative writing based on group analysis of a scene from *Mr. Smith Goes to Washington.*

Glatzer, Richard, and John Raeburn, eds. 1975. *Frank Capra: The Man and His Films.* Ann Arbor: University of Michigan Press.

This collection of important essays by critics and historians includes several revealing interviews with Capra.

Maland, Charles J. 1980. *Frank Capra.* Boston: Twayne.

A solid chronological treatment of Capra's films and reputation.

Questions for Discussion

1. Jefferson Smith believes in "the American way." How do we learn about his concept of America? Where did Smith get his views?

2. Smith's idealism contrasts sharply in the film with Taylor's ruthless despotism, Paine's pragmatic politics, and Saunders's wise-crack-

ing cynicism. Do you find Smith's patriotism corny and naive? Do you think it reflects the genuine spirit of American democracy?

3. When this film was released in 1939, Europe was at the brink of war. Do you see any evidence that Capra had the war in mind?

4. When Smith first visits the Lincoln Memorial, his thoughts are shown in a montage of images from American history and a medley of American songs. What abstract concepts do those images and songs evoke? How successful is the montage in picturing these concepts?

5. Throughout the film, we learn about the workings of American democracy, both ideal and actual. At one point, Saunders tells Smith how a bill becomes a law. At another time, a radio announcer explains the filibuster. How accurate are these explanations? What purposes do they serve?

6. *Mr. Smith* is filled with images of Washington, D.C. How many did you recognize? Do you see any changes in the way these images appear as the film progresses? What overall impression of the nation's capital are we left with at the end of the film?

7. Trace Smith's view of Senator Paine, the "Silver Knight." At what point does his view begin to change? How does Capra show this change? What does Paine's final confession reveal about himself, about Smith, and about the nature of politics in America?

8. In recent times, there has been a number of inquiries into the ethical behavior of government officials. Choose one and compare it to Smith's situation.

9. The corrupt political boss is a recurring figure in American films. There is Jim Gettys in *Citizen Kane*. There is Johnny Friendly in *On the Waterfront*. Compare these figures to Jim Taylor. Where do we find comparable figures in today's movies? How do modern audiences regard them?

Topics for Further Study

1. Capra's views about the film and larger issues are available in his autobiography and several interviews. Investigate Capra's career and philosophy. How does an inside view of the director enrich—or interfere with—the experience of watching his films?

2. When *Mr. Smith Goes to Washington* was released, World War II

had broken out in Europe. How would you expect the film to be received at that time? Read about the film's reception in 1939, and report on the actual response of general audiences and critics.

3. Scenes to analyze:

- The governor's family at supper.
- Smith meets Susan Paine at Union Station.
- The wordless "liberty" montage and medley of American songs.
- Lincoln Memorial.
- Smith meets the press.
- Saunders explains how a bill becomes a law.
- Smith filibusters at the Senate.
- Taylor's machine strikes home.
- Paine's confession on the Senate floor.

12 The Grapes of Wrath

Directed by John Ford; based on the novel by John Steinbeck; produced by Darryl F. Zanuck; script by Nunnally Johnson; cinematography by Gregg Toland; art direction by Richard Day and Mark Lee Kirk; edited by Robert Simpson; set design by Thomas Little; music by Alfred Newman; released by Twentieth Century-Fox in 1940. [129 minutes]

Tom Joad	*Henry Fonda*
Ma Joad	*Jane Darwell*
Pa Joad	*Russell Simpson*
Casy	*John Carradine*
Muley Graves	*John Qualen*
Grampa	*Charley Grapewin*
Granma	*Zeffie Tilbury*
Al	*O. Z. Whitehead*
Rosasharn	*Dorris Bowdon*
Connie	*Eddie Quillan*
Uncle John	*Frank Darien*

Filmed in 1940, *The Grapes of Wrath* documents the spirit of a decade. The Great Depression of the 1930s had hit farmers particularly hard. One reason was the decline of tenant farming, which once enabled families to work on modest plots of land. As farm machines became more practical, larger farms could be managed with fewer workers. This meant a shift from family to corporate ownership. Other reasons lay in unsound farming practices and in bad luck. For years the soil had been used without replenishment, while a devastating drought in 1934 turned much of the Great Plains into a "dust bowl," forcing thousands to leave their ancestral homes. Lured by the promise of work in California, these migrants arrived in droves and found massive poverty and unemployment instead of the promised land.

John Steinbeck was deeply moved by these conditions:

> I must go over to the interior valleys. There are about five thousand families starving to death over there, not just hungry but actually starving. The government is trying to feed them and get medical attention to them with the fascist group of utilities and banks and huge growers sabotaging the thing all along the line and yelling for a balanced budget.... I've tied into the thing from the first

and I must get down there and see it and see if I can't do
something to help knock these murderers on their heads. (Beja
1979b, 111)

John Steinbeck (1902–68), born and educated in California, had
already completed several books when he wrote this in a letter to his
literary agent in 1938. *Tortilla Flat* (1935) celebrated the simple life of
poor Hispanics. *In Dubious Battle* (1936) dramatized the plight of labor
organizers among California's fruit-pickers. *Of Mice and Men* (1937)
told the story of two migrant workers, a giant half-wit and his protective
friend. In the late 1930s, Steinbeck was especially impressed by the
documentary films of Pare Lorentz, which starkly depicted the social
and economic causes of the Depression on the screen. The visual
power of Lorentz's films as well as their rhythmic narrative style had
a noticeable influence on Steinbeck's writing, especially in *The Grapes
of Wrath*. Steinbeck's sympathy for the oppressed, rooted in personal
experience and articulated in his early novels, became even more
sharply focused, as if the story were seen at times through the lens
of documentary cinema. The book's conversion to a movie seemed a
natural step.

The novel, widely considered to be Steinbeck's masterpiece, was
completed in 1939. Against the backdrop of the Depression, corporate
greed, and massive deprivation, it focused on one family of tenant
farmers, the Joads. Theirs is the story of dispossession, migration,
humiliation, an almost epic quest for work and human dignity. The
book was an immediate popular and critical success, topping the
bestseller list for two years. But it also aroused fierce opposition,
particularly among agricultural groups in California, where the book
was denounced, banned, even burned as Communist propaganda.

It seems ironic, then, that the director charged with turning Steinbeck's book into a movie would be John Ford. Ford (1895–1973) was
regarded as a commercial filmmaker, known for war movies (*The Lost
Patrol*, 1934), musicals (*Steamboat 'Round the Bend*, 1935), and Westerns
(*Stagecoach*, 1939). While he sometimes took on social issues (*The
Informer*, 1935), his views seemed more conservative than radical. The
central focus in his films, he said, was on "individuals . . . face-to-face
with something bigger than themselves. The situation, the tragic
moment, forces [them] to reveal themselves, and to become aware of
what they truly are" (Beja 1979b, 109).

Ford received four Academy Awards for his directing. His bountiful
career spanned fifty years of steady film production and several
generations of Hollywood genres. Despite the peaks and valleys,
Andrew Sarris included him in his pantheon of great directors. "Ford,"

wrote Sarris, "is more than the sum of his great moments. A storyteller and a poet of images, he made his movies both move and moving" (1968, 49).

The Grapes of Wrath was filmed in secret, under a false title (*Highway 66*) and in studios instead of in the California valley, to avoid disruption by political pressure groups. Although Ford claimed that he never read the book, the film follows Steinbeck's novel remarkably. Edmund Wilson observed that Steinbeck's stories often transfer easily to the screen because the author rarely enters the consciousness of his characters (Bluestone 1957b, 147). The problem, however, is not so much how to represent their inner lives, but how to translate Steinbeck's broad generalizations into cinematic images. Nunnally Johnson's script omits the sixteen interchapters which contain the author's polemics on commerce, politics, and biological determinism. Instead, it concentrates on the Joads. In place of an indictment of corporate ownership, we see a bulldozer smashing through a family home. In place of an angry commentary on displaced migrants, we see Ma Joad silently selecting a few sentimental objects from her hope chest. Aside from leaving out the interchapters, the film generally follows the novel's major episodes, maintaining roughly the same order and ratio. However, as George Bluestone points out, the ending is significantly altered. Whereas the novel concludes with the disastrous strike (Tom is beaten, Casy killed, the strikers defeated), the film ends with the Government Camp sequence and a line from Chapter XX: "We'll go on forever, Pa. We're the people" (1957b, 147–69). The final effect is to make the film more optimistic than the book. Bluestone also notes a thematic displacement, from the need for radical reform to the value of passive persistence (1957b, 167). The spotlight thus shifts from the oppression of the workers to the enduring values of family. The legal authorities are exempt from blame; the religious satire is absent. Steinbeck's political point is blunted. Instead, as Warren French observes, Ford's film offers an essentially conservative faith in character and community (1973, 38).

As with most films, the achievements of *The Grapes of Wrath* are attributable to more than one person. The camera work is by Gregg Toland. In contrast to the self-conscious cinematic effects which Toland obtained a year later in *Citizen Kane*, Toland's camera here remains detachedly respectful of its subject, much as Walker Evans's still photographs of the 1930s in *Let Us Now Praise Famous Men* (1941) differ from the artfully intrusive shots in Bourke-White's *You Have Seen Their Faces* (1937). But Toland's use of low-key lighting is already evident in Ford's film. Nearly half the scenes are at night, when deep shadows cast figures and faces into sharp relief—and hide imperfections in the set. The musical score is by Alfred Newman, whose variations on "Red River Valley" infuse the film with a sentimental flavor of tradition. Much of the acting may seem stereotyped today, but two performances are often singled out: Henry Fonda's low-key portrayal of Tom Joad aptly complements Toland's photography; and Jane Darwell won an Academy Award for her supporting role as Ma Joad.

Steinbeck received a Pulitzer Prize for the novel in 1940, the year Ford received an Academy Award for the film. In the same year, Lewis Milestone directed Steinbeck's *Of Mice and Men*. Other works by Steinbeck have been adapted for the screen, including Victor Fleming's *Tortilla Flat* (1942), Irving Pichel's *The Moon Is Down* (1943), Elia Kazan's *East of Eden* (1955), and David S. Ward's *Cannery Row* (1982). Three adaptations, Emilio Fernandez's *The Pearl* (1946), Lewis Milestone's *The Red Pony* (1949), and Elia Kazan's *Viva Zapata!* (1952) were based on Steinbeck's own screenplays.

Suggested Films and Readings

More Films by John Ford

> *The Lost Patrol* (1934)
>
> *The Informer* (1935)
>
> *Steamboat 'Round the Bend* (1935)
>
> *The Plough and the Stars* (1936)
>
> *Stagecoach* (1939)
>
> *Young Mr. Lincoln* (1939)
>
> *Drums along the Mohawk* (1939)
>
> *How Green Was My Valley* (1941)
>
> *The Battle of Midway* (1942)
>
> *My Darling Clementine* (1946)
>
> *The Quiet Man* (1952)
>
> *The Searchers* (1956)
>
> *The Man Who Shot Liberty Valance* (1962)

Books about John Steinbeck, John Ford, and The Grapes of Wrath

Beja, Morris. 1979. *"The Grapes of Wrath."* In *Film & Literature: An Introduction.* New York: Longman. 107–117.

Beja's section on Ford's film contains useful background information and topics for discussion.

Bluestone, George. 1957b. "*The Grapes of Wrath.*" In *Novels into Film.* Baltimore: Johns Hopkins Press. 147–69.

An intelligent, methodical comparison of the novel and the film.

Bogdanovich, Peter. 1968. *John Ford.* Berkeley: University of California Press. New revised and enlarged edition, 1978.

Interviews with John Ford by a noted critic and director.

French, Warren, ed. 1972. *A Companion to* The Grapes of Wrath. New York: Viking.

Critical essays and background on the novel.

———. 1973. *Filmguide to* The Grapes of Wrath. Bloomington: Indiana University Press.

A thorough analysis of the film and its relation to the screenplay as well as Steinbeck's novel.

Gallagher, Tag. 1986. *John Ford: The Man and His Films.* Berkeley: University of California Press.

One of the most recent and important biographies of the director and his work.

Johnson, Nunnally. 1943. "*The Grapes of Wrath.*" In *Twenty Best Film Plays*, edited by John Gassner and Dudley Nichols. New York: Crown. 333–337.

The original screenplay.

Steinbeck, John. 1989. *Working Days: The Journals of* The Grapes of Wrath, *1938–1941.* Edited by Robert DeMott. New York: Viking.

———. 1939. *The Grapes of Wrath.* New York: Penguin Books.

Questions for Reflection and Discussion

1. Steinbeck's novel *The Grapes of Wrath* enjoyed high critical and popular success when it appeared in 1939, yet it was denounced by pubic officials, banned, and even burned. What reasons can you see for such a strong negative reaction?

2. Filming a great novel is always a risk, since the story has already been told so well through the medium of written language. How does the experience of reading Steinbeck's novel compare to the

experience of watching Ford's film adaptation? If you prefer one to the other, how do you account for your preference?

3. Some of the most telling scenes in this film are without words, like the scene of Ma Joad bidding farewell to her mementos alone. Compare one such scene to its counterpart in Steinbeck's novel. How are the resources of cinema used to express feelings which the novelist conveys through written language?

4. People often remember individual images from this film, like the opening shot of Tom against the sky, or the Joads' overburdened truck on Highway 66. Which images do you find most memorable? What makes them so striking?

5. Along the highway from Oklahoma to California, the Joads encounter truck drivers, waitresses, gas station attendants, and other people of the road. How do these people respond to the family? What do their responses say about human nature?

6. As the film progresses, the Joad family suffers many losses. How does each loss affect the family as a group? Do these losses make the Joads stronger or weaker by the end?

7. At what point in the film does Ma begin to see that her family belongs to a larger community? When does Tom begin to understand this fact? What statement does the film make about the relationship about the individual's place in society?

8. Do you consider this a political film? Analyze a few specific scenes to explain your view.

9. Near the end of the film, Ma Joad says, "We'll go on forever, Pa. We're the people." What does she mean? Does the film support her belief?

10. Gregg Toland, the photographer for *Citizen Kane*, was responsible for the camera work and lighting of *The Grapes of Wrath*. How does his photography contribute to the mood of this film?

Topics for Further Study

1. Read about the film's reception and report on the controversy.

2. George Bluestone and Warren French have each compared the theme and structure of the novel to the film, arriving at quite different conclusions. Read their arguments (Bluestone, *Novels into Film*, pp. 147–69; French, *Filmguide to* The Grapes of Wrath, pp. 22–27) and decide which analysis is most convincing.

3. *The Grapes of Wrath* was filmed in 1940 at the close of the Depression. Read about the "Okies," migrant farming, strikes, and other economic conditions that shaped the lives of so many people in the 1930s. How are these conditions reflected in the film?

4. *Of Mice and Men,* another Steinbeck novel, was filmed in 1940 by Lewis Milestone. View the film and compare it to *The Grapes of Wrath.* What common themes emerge from the comparison? What other evidence can you see that both films are based on Steinbeck stories?

5. Scenes to analyze:

   - Tom meets Casy on the road.
   - The demolition of Muley's shack.
   - The Joads learn about California from a returning migrant.
   - Casy's prayer at grandpa's grave.
   - Compare the Hooverville Camp with the Government Camp.
   - Analyze the attack on Casy.
   - Tom's last talk with Ma Joad.
   - Ma Joad's last speech in the film.

13 Modern Times

*Produced, written, and directed by Charles Chaplin;
assistant directors: Carter De Haven and Henry Bergman; photographed by Rolland H. Totheroh and Ira
Morgan; edited by Charles Chaplin; music by Charles
Chaplin; musical direction by Alfred Newman; released
by United Artists in 1936. [89 minutes]*

A Tramp	Charles Chaplin
A Gamine	Paulette Goddard
Café Proprietor	Henry Bergman
Mechanic	Chester Conklin
Big Bill	Stanley Sanford
Worker/Burglar	Hank Mann
Worker/Burglar	Louis Natheaux
Company President	Allan Garcia
J. W. Biddle	Murdock MacQuarrie
Juvenile Officer	Wilfred Lucas
Tramp's Cellmate	Richard Alexander
Assembly Worker	Heinie Conklin
Prison Governor	Lloyd Ingraham
Prison Chaplin	Dr. Cecil Rhodes
Minister's Wife	Mira McKinney
Turbine Operator	Sammy Stein
Sheriff Couler	Stanley Blystone
Gamine's Sister	Gloria DeHaven

Students who rediscover the delights of silent cinema often are
surprised to learn how entertaining the old films can be. They are also
fascinated by the silent screen's greatest entertainer. At the age of
twenty-seven, Charlie Chaplin (1889–1977) was not merely the country's best-known film personality, he was "the most popular man in
the world." His speechless "little tramp" entertained millions around
the globe in a language that transcended cultural barriers. With some
second-hand props and a vigorous imagination, he developed comic
pantomime into a first-rate art.

Born in London, Chaplin was the child of vaudeville entertainers
who separated when he was a year old. After his father's death and
his mother's breakdown, when he was five years old, young Chaplin
and his brother were sent to an orphanage for destitute children. At

the age of eight, he joined a group of child performers called the Eight Lancaster Lads. Gradually, he earned a reputation for his comic music-hall routines. While on tour in the United States with the famous Fred Karno company, he was spotted by Mack Sennett, who signed him up for Keystone in 1913. It was the beginning of a screen career that spanned more than eighty films.

At Keystone, Chaplin soon adopted the baggy pants, bowler hat, mustache, and cane which were to become the trademarks of his movie image, but he was temperamentally unsuited for Sennett's frenetic comedies. Charlie was more interested in character, in social themes. Comedy for him was a way to comment on the world. As he began to make independent films, his style grew more distinctive. The tramp figure, which he invented for the screen, was in many ways an outgrowth of his personal life: the outsider who wants what others have—money, status, love—but never quite fits in. He shuffles between heroism and pathos.

From humble beginnings, Chaplin himself achieved unprecedented success. By 1933, his taxable assets were the highest in the country and he was the best-loved actor and director in the business. Yet his later life was clouded by depression, loneliness, and exile. Four marriages and a paternity suit produced a public outcry. His political statements caused a steady stream of protest by right-wing groups, from the American Legion to Senator Joseph McCarthy's House Un-American Activities Committee. In 1952, when accused of Communist affiliations, Chaplin left America vowing never to return. It was twenty years before he did return, to accept an Oscar, a few years before his death.

Modern Times is the little tramp's farewell. While the film has a sound track, it avoids true voice synchronization. Believing that the Tramp should never speak, Chaplin stresses instead the alien, mechanical nature of sound on film. What we hear is the automated voice of a feeding machine or the electronic voice accompanying an image of Big Brother in the factory. When the Tramp does speak, or rather sings, it is in an imaginary language. "Just sing," his partner says. "Forget the words."

In many ways, *Modern Times* is a movie of the 1930s. Its concerns are those of the Depression—poverty, hunger, unemployment. Chaplin was deeply interested in economics. He proposed a method for revaluing gold, supported Roosevelt's New Deal, and made a broadcast in 1933 backing the National Recovery Act. Even so, the film is more of an emotional response than an economic or political analysis of the times. The Tramp is not a leader of the masses, but an individual caught up in problems larger than himself. When he pauses to scratch himself on the assembly line, he disrupts the entire factory. When he tries to return a red flag fallen from a truck, he is arrested for leading a Communist rally. The consequences of these innocent, amusing acts are serious, though, reflecting issues in society at large.

Much of Chaplin's humor is directed at American institutions. The factory illustrates America's obsession with time and with automated labor. It is a place where men are engulfed by their own machines. In one scene, a mechanic (Chester Conklin) is caught in the machinery at lunchtime and must be fed while he lies half-swallowed by the gears and sprockets. In another scene, the Tramp is made to test an automatic feeding machine. Designed to save time, it tips soup into his mouth, offers him corn on a rolling cob, and wipes his lips with a stop-motion napkin pad. But the machine goes haywire, revving up the corn, dumping soup into his lap, and pummeling him with repeated applications of the napkin. The prison is a variation on this theme of automation, a place where men march between the lunch room and their cells in regimented columns. Once again, the Tramp is out of step. After sprinkling "nose powder" in his soup, he disrupts the prison's regimen of law and order, but he also saves the day. As a reward, he is given his freedom, but the outside world of frenzied streets and economic woes is frightening. "I like it here," he says, preferring to return to the security of prison.

The film's second part introduces the Gamine, played by Paulette Goddard. Like Chaplin, Goddard had come from a broken home and was forced to become her family's breadwinner as a child. She plays a similar role in *Modern Times*. The Tramp helps her escape from the police when she is caught stealing bread for her hungry siblings, and they fall in love. (Chaplin and Goddard had been secretly married before the film's release.) Together they fantasize about a cozy home where fruit grows just outside the window and an obliging cow stops by to offer milk, and their adventures in a department store and restaurant give Chaplin more opportunities to comment on American institutions. Fittingly, the only job he's suited for is entertainment. As the singing waiter who forgets the lyrics, he gives one of his most hilarious performances. It is the Tramp's last act, his swan song. It is also the end of an era. When the Gamine and the Tramp walk side-by-side toward the horizon, it is not along a dusty road but down a modern highway.

Suggested Films and Readings

More Films by Charlie Chaplin

> *The Tramp* (1915)
> *Easy Street* (1917)

The Immigrant (1917)

The Kid (1921)

The Gold Rush (1925)

City Lights (1931)

Modern Times (1936)

The Great Dictator (1940)

Monsieur Verdoux (1947)

A Countess from Hong Kong (1967)

Books about Charlie Chaplin and Modern Times

Chaplin, Charles. 1975. *My Life in Pictures*. New York: Grosset & Dunlap.

Chaplin narrates this photographic essay of his personal and professional life.

Robinson, David. 1985. *Chaplin: His Life and Art*. New York: McGraw-Hill.

Robinson's biography chronicles the minutiae of Chaplin's career while filling some important gaps in the record.

Maland, Charles J. 1989. *Chaplin and American Culture: The Evolution of a Star Image*. Princeton, N.J.: Princeton University Press.

Maland takes up the relationship between Chaplin and America: the changing social climate which nourished his unprecedented rise to stardom and the events which stained his public image.

McCaffrey, Donald W., ed. 1971. *Focus on Chaplin*. Englewood Cliffs, N.J.: Prentice-Hall.

Collected essays on the artist and his films.

Questions for Reflection and Discussion

1. The movie opens with this title superimposed over a clock face: " 'Modern Times.' A story of industry, of individual enterprise—humanity crusading in the pursuit of happiness." How seriously does Chaplin take these words? What does the film tell us about modern times?

2. *Modern Times* is Chaplin's first movie to use sound, but in many ways it is still a silent film. How does Chaplin use sound effects

and words to comment on the role of sound in film as well as to support the movie's themes?

3. Many students who have never watched a Chaplin film are genuinely delighted by his sense of humor. Which scenes do you find particularly funny? What makes them so entertaining?

4. *Modern Times* gives us various views of social institutions: a factory, a prison, a department store, the city. It also presents several figures of authority, like the factory boss, the preacher, the prison warden, and the police. What attitudes are conveyed toward these figures and institutions? To what extent is the film a social or political statement?

5. Consider the figure of the Tramp. Why does he keep getting into trouble? What does he want in life? How successful is he in the end?

6. Automation is a persistent problem in this film. The factory is automated. Prisoners are treated like automatons. The Tramp tries out an automatic feeding machine. What other references can you find to machines? According to the film, what are the consequences of this mechanization for humanity?

7. Food is another persistent motif. In the Gamine's first appearance, she is stealing food. In prison, the Tramp gets into trouble during lunchtime. In the factory, a mechanic is swallowed by his own machine and has to be fed while he is in its bowels. How else is food represented in the film? How do you account for this emphasis on eating?

8. The sound track of *Modern Times* carries musical themes from several songs, including "Hallelujah, I'm a Bum," "Prisoner's Song," "How Dry I Am," and "In the Evening by the Moonlight." To what purpose are they used?

9. Structurally, some critics see this movie as a loosely knit sequence of two-reelers. Others find broader, consistent patterns in Chaplin's arrangement of the scenes. What structural patterns do you see in the film? How carefully constructed is it?

Topics for Further Study

1. Charlie Chaplin was one of the most famous figures of his day, not only in America but in the entire world. Read about his reputation during the heyday of the silent movies, and try to account for his enormous popularity.

2. Later in his career, Chaplin's reputation suffered a decline. His popularity dropped, he was attacked by various pressure groups, and he left the country vowing never to return. Investigate the circumstances leading to Chaplin's self-imposed exile. What do they reveal about the climate of America during those times and the fate of individual artists like Chaplin?

3. Scenes to analyze:
   - The opening montage of sheep and men.
   - The Tramp on the assembly line.
   - The Bellows Feeding Machine.
   - The Tramp leads the street demonstration.
   - The Tramp and the preacher's wife.
   - The dream house.
   - The Singing Waiter.

14 The Birds

Directed and produced by Alfred Hitchcock; screenplay by Evan Hunter; based on the story by Daphne du Maurier; technicolor photography by Robert Burks; special effects by Lawrence A. Hampton; art direction by Robert Boyle and George Milo; editing by George Tomasini; birds trained by Ray Berwick; released by Universal in 1963. [120 minutes]

Mitch Brenner.	*Rod Taylor*
Melanie Daniels.	*Tippi Hedren*
Lydia Brenner	*Jessica Tandy*
Annie Hayworth	*Suzanne Pleshette*
Cathy Brenner.	*Veronica Cartwright*
Mrs. Bundy	*Ethel Griffies*
Sebastian Sholes.	*Charles McGraw*
Mrs. MacGruder	*Ruth McDevitt*

Alfred Hitchcock (1899–1980) liked to tell a story about his first encounter with the law:

> I must have been about four or five years old. My father sent me to the police station with a note. The chief of police read it and locked me in a cell for five or ten minutes, saying, "This is what we do to naughty boys." (Truffaut 1967, 17)

Hitchcock's story, in one form or another, is re-enacted in many of his films. An ordinary person, someone with whom the viewer can identify, is caught in extraordinary circumstances, often treated as a criminal or spy. When bad things happen to decent people, we begin to wonder what lies beneath the veil of decency. This is one of Hitchcock's most persistent themes.

As a child, Hitchcock was a loner. Quiet and generally well-behaved, he played mostly by himself, inventing his own games. In college, he studied engineering and art, interests which persist in the technical and visual preoccupations of his films. In interviews, he talks about his early fascination with the movies, how he devoured the cinematography journals and frequented the local theaters. Entering the film

industry in 1920 as a title designer, he worked his way up to directing by 1925. *The Lodger* (1926), titled in the United States as *The Case of Johnathan Drew,* contained many of the hallmarks of his visual style and introduced the motif of a man pursued for a crime he did not commit. It was also in *The Lodger* that Hitchcock filled in briefly when an extra was needed on the set, making the first of those screen appearances which became his personal signature. In *Blackmail* (1929), Hitchcock orchestrated a climactic pursuit over the rooftops of the British Museum, the first of many landmark chase scenes which include the Statue of Liberty (*Saboteur,* 1942), London's Royal Albert Hall (*The Man Who Knew Too Much,* 1934, 1956), and Mount Rushmore (*North By Northwest,* 1959). But he could also confine his action, as he did in *Lifeboat* (1944), where nearly the entire film takes place in a small boat. In time, Hitchcock became less interested in the plausibility of his stories than in creating a mood. As the "Master of Suspense," he came to rely on the "MacGuffin," his term for a plot device which is important only for its importance to the characters, like the secret formula in *The Thirty-Nine Steps* (1935). It merely motivates the action (Truffaut 1967, 98). By the 1950s, Hitchcock had reached directorial maturity with thrillers like *Rear Window* (1954) and *Vertigo* (1958).

After the immense success of *Psycho* in 1960, he decided to produce a different kind of horror film. The idea for a film about killer birds came from a short story by Daphne du Maurier, published in 1952. Du Maurier's story is set in the English countryside, where the birds begin their attack, which spreads to London and beyond. Hitchcock shifted the location to San Francisco and a small town named Bodega Bay.

Hitchcock is known as a director who puts his most creative effort into creating the shooting script. Once the script is written, shooting is largely a matter of following it. Since it is hard to cajole seasoned talent into rigid roles, Hitchcock often employed inexperienced actors. In *The Birds,* Jessica Tandy was the only veteran performer, while Suzanne Pleshette was a newcomer and Rod Taylor had not yet played his first major part. For the role of Melanie, Hitchcock selected Tippi Hedren, a professional model. He had seen her in a television commercial, a cool blonde smiling as a male admirer appreciatively whistles. The smile and the whistle became part of the film.

The main actors, however, are the birds. Donald Spoto tells how Ray Berwick trained hundreds of gulls, crows, and ravens for the film (1983, 490). Mechanical birds were created for scenes involving children. Animation, mattes, composite shots—all the tricks of the trade were used. Nearly four hundred shots, about one-quarter of those planned for the film, involved some kind of technical effect. The film's setting thus alternates between expansive outdoor locations and claustrophobic sets. Production designer Robert Boyle said he was inspired by a painting, *The Scream*, Edvard Munch's haunting image of loneliness and terror.

Critics have given various explanations of the birds. Robin Wood (1965) considers and rejects three popular interpretations: (1) that the birds take revenge on those who have mistreated them, (2) that the birds are God's punishment for humanity's evil, and (3) that the birds express tensions among the characters. He proposes that the birds are "a concrete embodiment of the arbitrary and unpredictable, of whatever makes human life and human relationships precarious, a reminder of fragility and instability . . . the possibility that life is meaningless and absurd" (126). Wood sees Melanie's sophistication as a disguise for her underlying insecurity; she is "imprisoned in a gilded cage of sophisticated triviality" (127). He observes that the birds are consistently identified with isolation, noting that Melanie's posture in the final attack is "a voluptuous surrender" (146).

The film's sexual undercurrents ripple throughout. Melanie and Mitch's mother, rivals in the story, appear uncannily alike. The mother looks to her son as a substitute for her dead husband. Annie, Mitch's former girlfriend, jokes about this attachment between mother and son, "with all due respect to Oedipus." No wonder, then, that *The Birds* is popular with Freudians. Margaret Horwitz interprets the birds' aggression as "a displacement for maternal possessiveness." According to Horwitz, "The birds function primarily as extensions of Lydia's hysterical fear of losing her son" (Deutelbaum 1986, 279). Bill Nichols (1987) has analyzed Freudian and Marxian readings of the cinematic text, focusing on "the intersection of sexual and ideological patterns of communication and exchange in the space between viewer and screen, reader and text" (1987, 134). Nichols sees Melanie's efforts to infiltrate the Brenner family as the locus of aggression. By invading the fragile relationship between mother and son, she invites attack. Nichols notes that violence is directed "at the window" (1987, 154), not only at characters in the story but also at the screen itself. Broken windows and spectacles link the spectacle of the film to the spectators. As viewers, we invade these private lives through voyeuristic acts. Like Melanie, we are punished for our transgressions.

Suggested Films and Readings

More Films by Alfred Hitchcock

> *The Lodger* (1926)
> *Blackmail* (1929)

The Man Who Knew Too Much (1934, 1955)

The Thirty-Nine Steps (1935)

Sabotage (1936)

Rebecca (1940)

Lifeboat (1944)

Notorious (1946)

Strangers on a Train (1951)

Rear Window (1954)

The Wrong Man (1956)

Vertigo (1958)

North by Northwest (1959)

Psycho (1960)

Frenzy (1972)

Books about Hitchcock and The Birds

Deutelbaum, Marshall, and Leland Poague, eds. 1986. *A Hitchcock Reader*. Ames: Iowa University Press.

Du Maurier, Daphne. [1967] 1982. "The Birds." In Alfred Hitchcock, ed., *Alfred Hitchcock's Spellbinders in Suspense*. Reprint. N.Y.: Random House.

This is the short story on which Hitchcock based his film.

LaValley, Albert J., ed. 1972. *Focus on Hitchcock*. Englewood Cliffs, N.J.: Prentice-Hall.

LaValley's collection includes interviews with the director, articles on the Hitchcock controversy, and critical essays on selected films.

Modleski, Tania. 1988. *The Women Who Knew Too Much: Hitchcock and Feminist Theory*. N.Y.: Methuen.

Modleski expands feminist theory of spectatorship and sexual difference by tracing the conflicts between Hitchcock's great need to control and the threatening power of women in his films—tensions which she sees as representative of an uneasy patriarchal authority.

Nichols, Bill. 1981. *Ideology and the Image: Social Representation in the Cinema and Other Media*. Bloomington: Indiana University Press.

Chapter 5 (pp. 133–69) offers a semiotic analysis of *The Birds* from Freudian and Marxist perspectives.

Rothman, William. 1982. *Hitchcock—The Murderous Gaze*. Cambridge, Mass.: Harvard University Press.

Rothman investigates the relationship between Hitchcock's camera and the viewer's gaze, focusing on themes of love and death. His approach combines close shot-by-shot analyses of selected films and broad philosophical meditations on the cinema.

Spoto, Donald. 1983. *The Dark Side of Genius: The Life of Alfred Hitchcock*. Boston: Little, Brown.

This chatty and meticulously detailed account of the director's career contains a long section on *The Birds*, in Chapter 13.

Taylor, John Russell. 1980. *Hitch: The Life and Times of Alfred Hitchcock*. N.Y.: Berkeley Publishing.

Taylor's informal, yet informative approach to Hitchcock's life and films, makes this early biography a comfortable, serviceable book to read.

Truffaut, François, with Helen Scott. *Hitchcock*. 1967. New York: Simon & Schuster.

A tribute in lively, informative interviews by one of France's great directors. Chapter 14 is on *The Birds*.

Wood, Robin. *Hitchcock's Films*. 1965. New York: Tantivy Press.

For many years, this was the standard study of Hitchcock. Chapter 6 is devoted to *The Birds*.

Questions for Reflection and Discussion

1. *The Birds* is considered by many to be a modern horror movie. What do you find particularly horrifying in the film? Compare the birds to the frightening creatures found in other films, like *King Kong* (1933), *Frankenstein* (1931), *Dracula* (1931), or *Moby Dick* (1956). What seems more terrifying: all those birds or a single, monstrous beast?

2. Trace the references to birds throughout the film: the lovebirds, the bird cage, chicken feed, and so on. What do we normally associate with birds? What do we usually think of them? How does the film play on these thoughts and associations?

3. Donald Spoto writes that *The Birds* "explores the fragility of human relationships and the fear of loss and abandonment" (1983, 487). What images of fragility, loss, or isolation do you remember from the film? Do you agree that Hitchcock is making a serious statement about human relations?

4. There is no music in this film. What takes its place? Select a scene where the sound track is particularly effective and explain why.

5. Various people in the film give explanations for the bird attacks. One sees them as harbingers of doomsday. Another blames Melanie for bringing this evil upon the town. A third speaks of humanity's mistreatment of nature. What reasons can you give? Do you think the film supports a consistent explanation for the events we see?

6. Describe Melanie's first appearance in the film. How do you feel about her at this point? Why? Account for any changes in your view of Melanie as the film progresses.

7. Some viewers notice a resemblance between Melanie and Lydia. How are they alike? What do they and Annie want from Mitch?

8. When Melanie and the Brenners board up their house against the birds, it is as if they were imprisoned in a cage. Compare their situation to the lovebirds from the pet shop. Do these people deserve what is happening to them?

9. Bill Nichols has observed that the film's violence is directed "at the window" (1981, 154). Birds attack glass windows, shatter eyeglasses, and peck at human eyes. The dialogue is filled with references to seeing. Given the fact that we experience the film as viewers, through the camera's voyeuristic lens, how can *The Birds* be interpreted as an assault on the audience?

10. When Annie describes Mitch's mother to Melanie, she adds, "With all due respect to Oedipus." What does she mean? How would you describe the relationship between Lydia and her son? How does this relationship account for Lydia's attitude toward Melanie? Do you think it is related to the birds?

11. The words, *The End*, do not appear at the conclusion of this film. What do you think will happen after Melanie and the Brenners drive away? What events in the film itself suggest this ending to you?

Topics for Further Study

1. The idea for *The Birds* came from a short story by Daphne du Maurier (1952). Hitchcock remembered the story after reading a newspaper report of massive bird attacks on a home in La Jolla, California (*Santa Cruz Sentinel*, 27 April 1960). On August 18 of

the next year, he read of another attack in the *Santa Cruz Sentinel*. Read Du Maurier's story or track down the news events and note the changes made in the film.

2. How does the beginning of the movie set the overall tone and feeling of the movie? Pay close attention to the credits, images, and sounds. Select a few shots from later in the film which intensify the feeling you describe.

3. More scenes to analyze:
   * Mitch and Melanie in the bird shop.
   * Melanie meets Mitch's mother.
   * The birds attack Cathy's party.
   * Lydia enters Fawcett's house.
   * Melanie on the school bench as the birds gather behind her.
   * People in the diner.
   * The birds attack Melanie in the attic.

15 Singin' in the Rain

Directed by Gene Kelly and Stanley Donen; produced by Arthur Freed; story and screenplay by Betty Comden and Adolph Green; musical numbers staged and directed by Gene Kelly and Stanley Donen; photographed by Harold Rosson; art direction by Cedric Gibbons and Randall Duell; edited by Adrienne Fazan; set decorations by Edwin B. Willis and Jacques Mapes; orchestrations by Conrad Salinger, Wally Heglun and Skip Martin; songs by Arthur Freed (lyrics) and Nacio Herb Brown (music); musical direction by Lennie Hayton; costumes by Walter Plunket; released by MGM in 1952. [103 minutes]

Don Lockwood	Gene Kelly
Cosmo Brown	Donald O'Connor
Kathy Selden	Debbie Reynolds
Lina Lamont	Jean Hagen
R. F. Simpson	Millard Mitchell
Zelda Zanders	Rita Moreno
Roscoe Dexter	Douglas Fowley
Dancer	Cyd Charisse
Dora Bailey	Madge Blake
Rod	King Donovan
Phoebe	Kathleen Freeman
Diction Coach	Bobby Watson
Sid Phillips	Tommy Farrell

Songs

Would You?
Singin' in the Rain
All I Do Is Dream of You
I've Got a Feeling You're Fooling
Wedding of the Painted Doll
Should I?
Make 'Em Laugh
You Were Meant for Me
You Are My Lucky Star
Fit as a Fiddle and Ready for Love
Good Mornin'
Moses

Who can forget the figure of Gene Kelly hanging from a lamppost with one hand, an umbrella folded in his other outstretched hand, broadly smiling skyward into the cascading rain? *Singin' in the Rain* (1952) is probably the best-known film of a perpetually popular American genre, the movie musical. It has everything Americans have come to expect from the genre: high-spirited acting, lavish costumes, memorable lyrics, and striking choreography. But the film has become a classic for another reason. It tells a story that movies love to tell: the autobiography of film. It is a nostalgic, self-satirizing story of Hollywood, by Hollywood, for Hollywood and its faithful fans.

It was produced by Arthur Freed, a man who produced more than forty celebrated musicals for MGM between 1939 and 1962. The heart of the film is a suite of successful songs written by Freed and Nacio Herb Brown during the 1920s and 1930s, before Freed was promoted to producer (Thomas 1974, 133). Their original "Singin' in the Rain" dates back to 1926 and was used for the grand finale in MGM's *Hollywood Review of 1929.* "Beautiful Girl," another number in the Freed-Brown catalog, had been sung by Bing Crosby in *Going Hollywood* (1933).

Betty Comden and Adolph Green were called in to write a script that would revolve around these songs. When they realized that all the numbers came from the period when Hollywood was converting from silents to talkies, they decided to write a comedy around that theme. It would be a lighthearted, satirical musical. At first, the idea was to build the plot around a singing cowboy, played by Howard Keel. As the musical concept grew, however, Keel was dropped in favor of someone with song-and-dance experience. That someone was Gene Kelly. Kelly had just finished *An American in Paris*, which was to win the Academy Award for best picture in 1951. He was reportedly delighted with the script (Comden and Green 1972, 8). Freed asked Kelly to direct and choreograph the film with Stanley Donen, who had worked with Kelly before as a dancer, co-choreographer, and co-director. It was a fortuitous formula.

The casting was no less fortunate. Kelly plays the role of Don Lockwood, a smug but charming screen idol who makes the switch from silents to talkies with the help of a talented ingenue with whom he falls in love. For the ingenue's part, Freed chose Debbie Reynolds, who really was just starting out in pictures. Donald O'Connor was cast as Kelly's comic sidekick. A veteran of vaudeville, O'Connor played the wise-cracking clown with acrobatic energy. For the role of Lina Lamont, the narcissistic silent star whose voice betrays her foolishness, Freed selected Jean Hagen, a seasoned screen actress. She was to win an Academy Award for her hilarious imitation of the quintessential 1920s vamp—Pola Negri, Norma Talmadge, and Jean Harlow rolled into one.

Comden and Green struggled with three different ideas for the opening. In one beginning, Lockwood and Lamont arrive at a movie premiere before a crowd of faithful followers. In another, Lockwood recounts his career for a radio interview. In the third, he meets an aspiring actress, Kathy Selden, and falls in love. All three ideas are combined in the final script. In a feat of narrative economy, Lockwood gives his interview at the premiere and jumps into Selden's passing car to escape his overzealous fans. Not only does this get the story moving, but it also sets the tone, theme, and historical background for the entire film. When Kelly talks about his rise to stardom, the camera contradicts his words. He speaks of studying the classics, and we see him as a boy sneaking in to see "The Dangers of Drusilla, Episode 12." He speaks about his Conservatory training, and we see him sawing the fiddle on Amateur Night. This dispute between appearance and reality, between what we see and what we hear, runs throughout the movie and fuels much of the fun.

However ludicrous, the extravagant premier and fabricated interview are not farfetched; they are standard Hollywood fare. Lockwood's biography—the real one, shown on film—follows the career of many musical performers. Kelly himself had worked his way up from digging ditches and pumping gas to road shows, vaudeville, Broadway, and Hollywood. In fact, a good deal of serious research went into authenticating the film's historical details. Walter Plunkett's costumes were duplicates of actual costumes he had made for 1920s films in the flapper days of beaded chiffon and monkey fur. Art director Randall Duell and set director Jacques Mapes built a replica of the old Chinese Theater, with its pit orchestra, to show how the silents were accompanied by live music. The film studio in which Lockwood and Lamont make their first "talkie" is based on old photographs, down to the bulky microphones, dubbing equipment, and glass-enclosed sound booth. Studios did hire diction coaches to help their silent stars make the transition, but Norma Talmadge's Brooklyn accent and John Gilbert's voice were beyond help. Like Lina Lamont, they never survived the transition.

From the moment sound becomes a factor, Lina is out of sync. Her voice doesn't match her looks; her self-image doesn't match what people see. This is the stuff of comedy. In some ways, it is the soul of comedy itself: an ironic contrast between what people seem and what they are. In *Singin' in the Rain*, the truth is sometimes in the image (Don's interview) and sometimes in the sound (Lina's voice). When Don and Lina act out a romantic scene for the silent *Duelling Cavalier,* the title cards speak love, but the actors are whispering words of venom to each other. When Lina is asked to give a live encore to her appreciative audience, Kathy Selden sings the song behind a curtain while Lina mouths the words. But life is funnier than fiction: In real life, Jean Hagen had a more cultivated voice than Debbie Reynolds, and when we see Kathy dubbing Lina's speaking voice, it is really Hagen dubbing Reynolds. Meanwhile, when Kathy pretends to sing for Lina, it is really another singer—Betty Royce—dubbing Reynolds, who is shown dubbing Hagen!

The movie musical is a distinctively American invention. It grew out of vaudeville and music-hall traditions in the late 1920s and early 1930s, reaching its peak by the 1940s. The stage musical is associated with Broadway, the nation's theater capital. *Show Boat,* the first musical play, opened there in 1927. In the same year, Warners released its first talkie, *The Jazz Singer,* also considered the first film musical (Schatz 1981, 187). But it was MGM's *Broadway Melody* (1929) that set the standards for screen musicals, winning the Oscar for best picture in 1928–29 and launching then lyricist Arthur Freed's remarkable career.

Over half of *Singin' in the Rain* (60 out of 103 minutes) is devoted to musical numbers. Although it is not unusual for musicals to alternate between the relatively static action of a story and the lively spectacle of song and dance, the transitions between story and spectacle may seem less forced in this film than in others, because the story is about making love and making movies. When Gene Kelly sings "You Were Meant for Me" to Debbie Reynolds, they are backstage, and he literally sets the stage for his romantic moment by switching on studio lights and a breeze machine. When O'Connor does his big comedy number, "Make 'Em Laugh," he illustrates his theme by dancing on, around, and through the props. The film's most ambitious number, "Broadway Melody-Broadway Rhythm," spoofs the extravagant 1930s productions of Busby Berkeley at the same time that it creates some genuinely moving, original effects. Cyd Charisse's performance as the city vamp is authentically bewitching, but her *pas de deux* with Kelly on a stage of pink and grey, with a gossamer scarf playing seductively between them in the wind, leaves the world of satire for a surrealistic otherworld. The central number is, of course, "Singin' in the Rain." Swinging his umbrella in an exuberant arch, bouncing from puddle to puddle, tossing his hat to the sky, Kelly expresses the joy of love that makes adults feel like children again. As playful and impromptu as it seems, the sequence was meticulously planned. Kelly had special holes drilled in the set so that each splash could be made at the right spot. The camera keeps pace with every step, like another dancer, moving in to catch his smile, tracking out to show his sweeping energy, craning up as he pirouettes around the lamppost. An exemplar of the film, of the whole musical genre, Kelly's "Singin' in the Rain" number captures the exuberant spirit of film as entertainment. More broadly, *Singin' in the Rain* affectionately spoofs its own cinematic origins. It makes fun of the industry which it celebrates and illustrates, Hollywood at its self-conscious best.

Suggested Films and Readings

More Films by Arthur Freed, Stanley Donen, and Gene Kelly

Although each had a flourishing independent career, the collaborations of Freed, Donen, and Kelly in various combinations produced some of the most memorable musicals in the genre:

> *Best Foot Forward* (1941)
>
> *For Me and My Gal* (1942)
>
> *Du Barry Was a Lady* (1942)
>
> *Ziegfeld Follies* (1946)
>
> *On the Town* (1948)
>
> *The Pirate* (1948)
>
> *Take Me Out to the Ball Game* (1949)
>
> *An American in Paris* (1951)
>
> *Royal Wedding* (1951)
>
> *Brigadoon* (1954)
>
> *It's Always Fair Weather* (1955)
>
> *Invitation to the Dance* (1967)

Books about Gene Kelly, Stanley Donen,
and the American Film Musical

Altman, Rick. 1987. *The American Film Musical*. Bloomington: Indiana University Press.

> This is probably the most authoritative, comprehensive book on the subject to date.

Altman, Rick, ed. 1986. *Genre, the Musical: A Reader*. London: Routledge

& Kegan Paul.

Altman's anthology offers a wide range of viewpoints on a much-discussed genre.

Casper, Joseph Andrew. 1983. *Stanley Donen*. Metuchen, N.J.: Scarecrow Press.

This film-by-film analysis of Donen's prolific career is full of pertinent facts and astute comments on each of his movies.

Comden, Betty, and Adolph Green. 1972. *Singin' in the Rain*. New York: Viking.

The published screenplay, introduced by the authors.

Feuer, Jane. 1982. *The Hollywood Musical*. Bloomington: Indiana University Press.

Feuer's dissertation has an academic tone and treats the subject more seriously than many of the popular books on musicals.

Schatz, Thomas. 1981. *Hollywood Genres: Formulas, Filmmaking, and the Studio System*. Philadelphia, Pa.: Temple University Press.

Chapter 7 gives a good general introduction to the American Musical.

Singin' in the Rain. 1988. Santa Monica, Calif.: The Criterion Collection.

This laserdisk recording of the film features an informative, entertaining "audio essay" by film historian Ronald Haver. Haver discusses the background of each scene on a second sound track. The disc includes archival material, such as the original promotion trailer, amusing outtakes, and earlier film versions of several songs.

Thomas, Tony. 1974. *The Films of Gene Kelly: Song and Dance Man*. Secaucus, N.J.: Citadel Press.

A lively photographic chronology of Kelly's life and film career.

Questions for Reflection and Discussion

1. When Don Lockwood gives his autobiographical interview, the film contradicts his words. When Lina Lamont talks on screen, her voice is dubbed by Kathy Selden. How many scenes in this movie are "out of sync"? What is the effect of this ironic contrast? How basic is it to the nature of comedy?

2. How is the history of motion pictures represented in the film? For example, how does it represent the popular attitudes toward

motion pictures of the 1920s and 1930s? What does it explain about the transition between silent movies and the talkies?

3. Audiences often laugh out loud during the movie. Who (or what) are they laughing at? To what degree is this a satire, a parody, or some other recognizable form of comedy?

4. Musicals typically alternate between dramatic scenes and musical numbers. Sometimes the drama seems stronger than the music; sometimes it's the other way around. How well integrated are story and spectacle in this film?

5. One strand of the plot is a backstage romance between Don Lockwood and Kathy Selden. Which dramatic scenes and musical numbers develop this theme? How do they fit into the structural and thematic design of the movie?

6. Some historians argue that the film musical reached its peak in the 1940s and has since lost its vitality. Do you agree? Give examples of contemporary musicals to support your point of view.

Topics for Further Study

1. Many of the people involved in making this movie were central figures in the history of American musicals, among them producer Arthur Freed, director Stanley Donen, dancer Gene Kelly, and costume designer Walter Plunkett. Find out more about any of these personalities and report on their careers.

2. Nearly all the songs in *Singin' in the Rain* are from earlier musicals. Some of the original performances are available as archival material on the laserdisc recording of the film, distributed by Janus Films. View these original performances and compare them to Kelly's interpretation of the songs.

3. The American film musical is one of Hollywood's great contributions to world cinema. Investigate the history of this genre. How did it begin, and what stages has it gone through? Compare *Singin' in the Rain* to earlier and later examples of the genre.

4. Scenes to analyze:
   • Don and Lina arrive at the premiere.
   • Don Lockwood tells the story of his life.
   • R. F. Simpson demonstrates the talking picture.
   • The sets of Monumental Studios.

- "Make 'em Laugh."
- 1930s musical montage.
- "Singin' in the Rain."
- "Broadway Melody/Broadway Rhythm."
- Selden dubs Lina onstage.

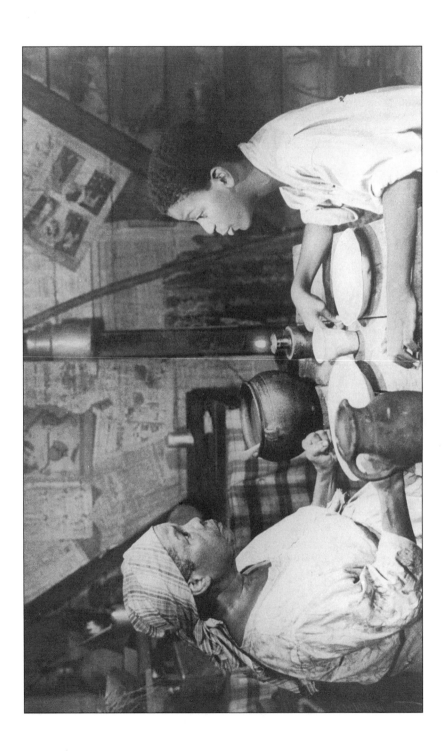

16 Sugar Cane Alley
(*Rue Cases Nègres*)

Directed by Euzhan Palcy; screenplay by Euzhan Palcy; based on the novel by Joseph Zobel; photography by Dominique Chapuis; edited by Marie-Joseph Yoyotte; music by Groupe Malavoix; produced by Sunafa-Orca; in French with English subtitles; released in 1983 by Orca Productions, Sunafra Productions, and NEF Diffusion. [103 minutes]

José.................................. *Garry Cadenat*
M'Man Tine .... *Darling Legitimus*
Médouze.............................. *Douta Seck*
Léopold .... *Laurent St. Cyr*
Monsieur St. Louis .... *Joby Bernabe*
Le Gereur........................ *Francisco Charles*
Léopold's Mother.................. *Marie-Jo Descas*
Léopold's Father.............. *Léon de la Guigneraye*
Madame St. Louis .... *Marie-Ange Farot*
Monsieur Roc .... *Henri Melon*
Douze Orteils .... *Eugène Mona*
Carmen.............................. *Joel Palcy*

It is the summer of 1930 in the small village of Rivière Salée. School is out, and the children wait impatiently for their parents to return to the cane fields so they can be left free for the day. Being children, they boast, play, tussle, and get into trouble. Being poor children of the West Indies, their boasting is about the codfish and bananas that they had for dinner; their playthings are grass charms, a snake, a mongoose, and a hen's egg. At the day's end, a ragged line of labor-weary parents trudges home. Some are singing. One man plays a flute. An elderly black woman, her hands bandaged from the pain, has a present for her grandson, José. It is wrapped in an old newspaper. As José unwraps it, she asks him to read the newspaper aloud. He reads it carefully, an advertisement for women who want firmer breasts. José pastes the newspaper on a board that is already filled with scraps of newsprint, his homemade reader.

The opening of *Sugar Cane Alley* (1983) introduces us to the verities and incongruities of everyday life in Martinique. It is a life of interminable drudgeries, abiding hopes, and flashes of danger, a story told with warmth, humor, sensitivity, and deeply felt convictions about the people and their daily struggles. At the center of the story is José, a bright, eager-eyed schoolboy who is learning about his people, the world around him, and himself. From his grandmother, a pipe-smoking matriarch known in the village as M'Man Tine, he learns love and respect. She has brought him up after his mother's death, dividing her time between the cane fields and her well-scrubbed home. From an old man named Médouze, he learns about his African heritage: the long trail from political slavery to economic servitude, with its inevitable acceptance of oppression. "We were free," says the old man, "but our bellies were empty. The law forbids whites to beat blacks, but it doesn't force them to pay decent wages." José spends part of his time with Carmen, a handsome older boy whom he teaches to read and who dreams of becoming a Hollywood movie star. He also spends time with Léopold, the Mulatto son of a white plantation owner. One day, Carmen shows José the bed where he has been sleeping with the master's white wife. Another time, Léopold is disinherited by his dying father because the man will not give his white name to the child of his black mistress. Week by week, José learns the codes of color by which his people live.

Yet the story is not hopelessly bleak. José is an exceptionally talented student. He has a chance to win a scholarship to the Catholic school in Fort-de-France. Through determination and self-sacrifice, M'Man Tine gives him that chance, uprooting herself from the village to scrub clothes for wealthy people in the city. Their new home is a packing crate, but every day José moves closer to his goal. By the movie's end, José has learned much more about life and the world beyond his village. "I'll return to Fort-de-France," he promises, and he adds, "I'll take my Sugar Cane Alley with me."

Sugar Cane Alley is based on Joseph Zobel's autobiographical novel, first published in 1950. The book won the prestigious Prix des Lecteurs in Paris and eventually it became a national classic, read eagerly in schools throughout Martinique, Guadeloupe, and the African continent, especially Senegal, where Zobel had taught for ten years.

Euzhan Palcy had read it at the age of fourteen. A devotee of the movies, especially those of Fritz Lang, Orson Welles, Jean Renoir, François Truffaut, and Ousmane Sembene, she dreamed of bringing Zobel's story to the screen. She worked for Martinique television, studied literature and theater in Paris, and enrolled in the French film school, École de Vaugirard. At the age of 28, she was able to fulfill her dream with the completion of *Sugar Cane Alley*. Just as José returned to his roots at the novel's end, Palcy returned to Martinique to make her first major film. "My true entry into movies," she explained, "could only be through *Sugar Cane Alley*" (Micciollo 1983, 34). Since stepping through the gateway of her native streets into international acclaim, Palcy has remained true to her political vision. In 1989, she became the first black woman to direct a Hollywood feature with *A Dry White Season*, an intense and painful story of the Soweto uprisings in South Africa told from the viewpoint of a white Afrikaner. With a budget large enough to engage stars like Donald Sutherland and Marlon Brando, she was able to bring this story of racial injustice, political awakening, and moral courage to movie screens around the world. Students of film can learn a great deal by following Palcy's career as she enlarges both her vision and her audience.

Sugar Cane Alley was a great success in France and the United States. Reviewing the 1984 New Directors Festival in New York City, Vincent Canby thought Palcy's debut was "as important as any in the festival's thirteen years of existence." The French journal *Cinéaste* proclaimed, "it is almost impossible to praise her debut too highly" (De Stefano 1984, 44). Andrew Sarris called it "the work of a world-class filmmaker" (1984, 49). Canby compared the film to *How Green Was My Valley* (1941) and *The Corn is Green* (1945), believing it to be better made, "not because its locations are authentic, but because its passions are more raw and less cinematically genteel" (1984, 15). George De Stefano found it "profoundly political yet never didactic; emotionally wrenching yet humorous and essentially optimistic." (1984, 45). De Stefano stressed the film's fidelity to its West Indies origins: "the aspirations of Palcy's protagonist are rooted in the conditions of his people" (1984, 44). Sarris emphasized the movie's broad appeal, noting that Palcy "manages to transform a very painful third world subject into universally accessible humanist cinema" (1984, 50).

Only two actors in the film are professionals. Darling Legitimus plays M'Man Tine with gentle warmth and vigorous conviction. The role of Médouze is performed by the Senegalese actor, Douta Seck, who represents the soul of Africa with haunting composure. Together, M'Man Tine and Médouze are José's spiritual parents. He learns about the value of education and the power of storytelling from them. He also learns about love, respect, and self-esteem. Palcy chose the rest of the cast from the sugar cane alleys of Martinique. "My actors didn't have to act but to reinterpret their lives," she said in an interview (Micciollo 1983, 34). The result is an artlessly convincing, almost documentary quality that pervades the entire film.

Palcy photographs much of the movie in sepia tones that soften its political dichotomies and lend an aura of nostalgia. The French critic Henri Micciollo also sees thematic implications in this photographic technique. By using beiges, browns, and greens instead of pure white or stark black, "the film translates into its aesthetic system a fundamental theme of negritude: only the fact of interiorizing black (to make it a force) permits comparison with white" (1983, 32). Micciollo also notes that José's school uniform is white, while the lodging woman prevents him from getting to school on time by demanding that he polish her black shoes. Elsewhere, the shades of black and white are more subtle. Palcy is attentive to gradations within the black community itself, where a handsome black youth can boast of sleeping with his white missus and a black woman in a ticket booth can say, "Except for my color, I'm not black. My character is white."

Palcy dedicated her film to "all the Black Shack alleys of the world." Its story is about colonial repression and the arduous conditions of a people. Yet it is also the story of a boy's coming of age, the story of an education, of the urgency of education. Through José's eyes and Palcy's camera, a much wider audience can learn to look with deeper understanding into the neglected corners of the globe.

Suggested Films and Readings

More Films of Special Interest

> *A Dry White Season* (1989) Euzhan Palcy, USA
>
> "The Battle of Chile" series (1975–79) Patricio Guzmán, Chile
>
> *Blood of the Condor* (1969) Jorge Sanjines, Bolivia
>
> *The Gods Must Be Crazy* (1983) Jamie Uys, Botswana
>
> *The Hour of the Furnaces* (1968) Fernando Solanas and Octavio Getino, Argentina
>
> *Kiss of the Spider Woman* (1985) Hector Babenco, Brazil
>
> *Xala* (1974) Ousmane Sembene, Senegal
>
> *Xica* (1976) Carlos Diegues, Brazil

Reviews of Sugar Cane Alley

Canby, Vincent. "Film View: Third World Truths from *Sugar Cane Alley.*" *The New York Times.* 22 April 1984: C15.

Coleman, John. "Films: Write Angles." *New Statesman.* 18 May 1984: 28.

Denby, David. Review. *New York.* 30 April 1984: 88–89.

De Stefano, George. 1984. Review. *Cinéaste* 23,4: 44–45.

Forbes, Jill. "Rue Cases Nègres (Black Shack Alley)." *Monthly Film Bulletin.* July 1984: 210–11.

Micciollo, Henri. "Rue Cases Nègres." *Cinéma.* Oct. 1983: 31–34.

Sarris, Andrew. "Oscar Hangover, Third-World Crossover." *The Village Voice.* 24 April 1984: 49–50.

Sterritt, David. "Two Films from Foreign Lands with Fresh Insights on Children." *Christian Science Monitor.* 26 April 1984: 29–30.

Related Readings

Armes, Roy. 1987. *Third World Film Making and the West.* Berkeley: University of California Press.

Burton, Julianne, comp. 1976. *The New Latin Cinema: An Annotated Bibliography of English-Language Sources, 1960–1976.* New York: Cinèaste.

Cyr, Helen W. 1976. *A Filmography of the Third World: An Annotated List of 16mm Films.* Metuchen, N.J.: Scarecrow.

Gabriel, Teshome H. 1982. *Third Cinema in the Third World: The Aesthetics of Liberation.* Ann Arbor: University of Michigan Press.

Pfaff, Françoise. 1984. *The Cinema of Ousmane Sembene; A Pioneer of African Film.* Westport, Conn.: Greenwood.

Zobel, Joseph. 1950. *Black Shack Alley.* Translated by Keith Warner. Washington, D.C.: Three Continents Press.

Questions for Discussion

1. *Sugar Cane Alley* has been called a "film of apprenticeship." Who are José's teachers, and what does he learn from each? How does this informal way of learning compare to his schoolhouse education?

2. Contrast the death scenes of M'Man Tine, Médouze, and Léopold's father. How is the mood of each scene created? How does this mood reflect the values which each character embodied during life?

3. The film is set in 1930. How does Palcy create a sense of the past? Consider the photography, music, and set design, including details like the recording of Josephine Baker and the poster of Al Jolson. What is gained by setting the story in the past?

4. Palcy dedicated her film to "all the Black Shack Alleys of the

world." What do you think she meant? To what degree does the film seem rooted in a particular place and time? To what degree does it seem universal?

5. Critics have commented on Palcy's use of black and white and all the shades between. How is shading used symbolically throughout the film?

6. None of the children and few of the adults in this movie had acted before. Do you consider their lack of professional experience a weakness or a strength of the film? Why?

7. Contrast José to the other young people in his village. What binds them together? What sets them apart? Describe the scenes in which these bonds and divisions are revealed most clearly.

8. The end of the school term marks a turning point in each child's life. How much depends on their education? How much depends on other circumstances? Compare the role of education in this film to its role elsewhere, including your own community.

9. This is a film in which objects have a voice: a watch, a wood carving, a hen's egg, or a pair of shoes tell us as much about people, conditions, and relationships as any dialogue. Which objects do you find particularly telling? Why?

10. At the end of the film, José says, "I'll return to Fort-de-France. I'll take my Sugar Cane Alley with me." How do you think he intends to keep his word?

Topics for Further Study

1. Palcy based her film on a prize-winning novel by the Martinique writer, Joseph Zobel. Read the book. How is the movie faithful to the spirit and details of Zobel's novel? What changes do you find most significant?

2. Of the twelve films featured in this book, *Sugar Cane Alley* is the only one with subtitles. How did the subtitles affect your response to the film? What other foreign movies have you seen? Compare them to Palcy's film.

3. *Sugar Cane Alley* is part of an emerging cinema of Third World countries. Find out more about the directors and film industries of these countries. What sets them apart from their counterparts in other lands? What ties them to the community of world cinema? What kind of future do you see for Third World cinema?

4. Scenes to Analyze:
   - The postcards that introduce the film.
   - The villagers return from the cane fields.
   - M'Man Tine brings José a gift wrapped in newsprint.
   - Payday.
   - The fire.
   - Médouze relates the story of his African ancestors.
   - Médouze's body is found in the fields.
   - Carmen introduces José to the house of his "missus."
   - Leonard's arrest.
   - José washes Grandma's feet.

17 Do the Right Thing

Produced, written, and directed by Spike Lee; co-producer, Monty Ross; photography by Ernest Dickerson; edited by Barry Alexander Brown; costumes by Ruthe Carter; original music score by Bill Lee; production design by Wynn Thomas; released by Universal Pictures in 1989. [120 minutes]

Sal.	Danny Aiello
Da Mayor	Ossie Davis
Mother Sister	Ruby Dee
Vito	Richard Edson
Buggin' Out	Giancarlo Esposito
Mookie	Spike Lee
Radio Raheem	Bill Nunn
Pino	John Turturro
ML	Paul Benjamin
Coconut Sid	Frankie Faison
Sweet Dick Willie	Robin Harris
Jade	Joie Lee
Officer Ponte	Miguel Sandoval
Officer Long	Rick Aiello
Clifton	John Savage
Tina	Rosie Perez
Smiley	Roger Smith
Hector	Travell Lee Toulson
Kim	Ginny Yang
Mister Señor Love Daddy	Sam Jackson

The availability of films on videotape has made it practical to study current films before they can be seen in the more expensive 16mm format. This brings the benefits—and problems—of screening contemporary issues closer to the classroom. Few recent films offer such rich subjects for study and discussion as Spike Lee's *Do the Right Thing* (1989). Here is a film that presents racial stereotypes while at the same time challenging them.

The film is set in a black neighborhood in Brooklyn, New York, on the hottest day of the year. In a twenty-four-hour period, we watch the community wake up to the music of WE LOVE radio, see folks greet each other on the street, and watch them congregate at Sal's Famous Pizzeria, the central setting of the film. As the day grows hotter and tempers flare, we witness a chain of events that builds up to a violent catastrophe.

From the beginning, the scene vibrates with a procession of memorable characters. We meet Mother Sister, who keeps a watchful eye on everything from her apartment window, and a good-hearted, ineffectual old man who calls himself "Da Mayor." We meet the Corner Men (ML, Coconut Sid, and Sweet Dick Willie), a trio of middle-aged ne'er-do-wells who comment on the passing scene from under their umbrella. We meet a frenetic provocateur named Buggin' Out, a tight-lipped youth called Radio Raheem, whose voice is in his boom box, and Smiley, the neighborhood mute, who hawks colorized photographs of Malcolm X and Martin Luther King. There are also Officers Long and Ponte, who cruise the street suspiciously in their patrol car. There are the Kims, who run a Korean grocery store. The cast includes more than fifty individuals.

The main characters are Sal and Mookie. Sal operates the pizzeria with his dimwitted sons, Vito and Pino. Mookie (played by Spike Lee) works there for $250 a week. Sal is more temperamental than bigoted. He is proud that the neighborhood has grown up on his food, but he becomes enraged when Buggin' Out insists that he should add photographs of African-Americans to his gallery of Italian personalities on the pizzeria's Wall of Fame. Mookie is witty and well-liked, but he is constantly berated by his sister and the girl who bore his child for his aimless irresponsibility. In his journal of film ideas that accompanies the published script, Lee wrote that "every character should have a function . . . should appear again and advance the script" (1989, 32), and that the block "should be a character in its own right" (1989, 29). This is just what happens. Everyone, not least of all the block itself, is caught up in the sweep of incidents that lead to death and destruction by the day's end.

Lee's conception of the film was shaped by actual events. He noted in his journal that the pizza parlor is a reference to Howard Beach, an incident in 1986 during which three black men were attacked in Queens, New York, by a white mob wielding baseball bats. The Louisville Slugger that Sal keeps behind his counter is an allusion to this incident, as is the action which precipitates mob violence in the film. When Mookie hurls a trash can into the pizzeria's window, he shouts "Howard Beach," and the crowd echoes his call with cries of "Coward Beach." During the film's planning, there was yet another incident of racial tension, this time in the Bensonhurst section of Brooklyn. Sal and his boys commute from Bensonhurst. But the film's imagery and emotional intensity point to a broader sweep of racial stresses and injustices: to Birmingham and Montgomery, to Malcolm X and Martin Luther King, to the whole tortured history of race relations in the United States.

Spike Lee was born in Atlanta in 1957, but he grew up in Brooklyn. His middle-class family encouraged artistic inclinations. Bill Lee, his father, was a musician (he wrote the film's music score). Spike Lee's sister Joie became an actress; she plays the role of Mookie's sister in the film. After graduating from Morehouse College, Lee went on to New York University's Film School, where his directing talents and focus on controversial social issues gained immediate attention. One of his student films, *Joe's Bed-Stuy Barbershop: We Cut Heads* (1982), is about a black numbers racketeer who wrests control of the local action from the Mafia. His first feature film, *She's Gotta Have It* (1986), takes up questions of racial and sexual stereotypes. In it, Lee reverses the usual gender roles by following a young black woman's sexual adventures with three men. In *School Daze* (1988), Lee trains his camera on student life in a black college, where skin tones are signs of intraracial prejudice. The chief conceptual conflict in this film is between assimilation, represented by a house of fraternity "wannabees," and Afrocentrism, represented by a group of anti-apartheid activists. Compounding the conflict is the issue of sexual politics between fraternities and sororities.

As in his other films, the story of *Do the Right Thing* is presented from a black perspective. Lee's journal keeps stressing this point of view but emphasizes his intention to avoid ethnic stereotypes (1989, 40, 45). In fact, the final film seems to have surpassed his intention. The police seem less corrupt than originally planned (1989, 28). The firemen appear less malicious (1989, 65). Sal himself, as played by Danny Aiello, isn't quite the racist he was meant to be; at least that is what emerges in a discussion between the actor and the director in St. Clair Bourne's documentary, *Making Do the Right Thing* (1989). Thomas Doherty sees this as an example of how an "actor can overwhelm an auteur" (1989, 38). In other ways Lee's strength as a director prevailed. His constant camera movement helps to create the momentum that he wanted (1989, 37). His use of diagonal shots (he calls them Chinese angles) increases the tension that he sought to build in certain scenes (1989, 51). His long takes are effectively choreographed. Some of the effects are acknowledged tributes to films that Lee admired, like *Night of the Hunter* (1955), *The Third Man* (1949), *In the Heat of the Night* (1967), *Body Heat* (1981), and *Apocalypse Now* (1979) (1989, 51, 78). But much of the film's power lies in its originality.

Few movies tell the story of an urban black community from its own point of view with such wit, energy, and sustained conviction.

Lee's production notes explain how he settled on the film's location, Stuyvesant Street between Lexington and Quincy Avenues, in the heart of the Bedford-Stuyvesant section of Brooklyn, "a community that has some of the highest unemployment, infant mortality, and drug-related homicides in New York City" (1989, 109). The notes tell how he hired a group of Black Muslims to patrol the set and shut down drug traffic in the area. These observations, together with the journal, offer a fascinating glimpse into the creative processes of planning and shooting a major motion picture. They describe the casting, rehearsals, costume decisions, financial obstacles, shooting problems (five days for the johnny pump [fire hydrant] scene, five takes before the trash can broke the window), daily screenings, editing, and final wrap. "When you're directing a film," Lee writes, "it takes over your life completely. You get up at the crack of dawn, shoot for twelve or fourteen hours (if you're lucky), watch dailies, grab something to eat before you go to bed, then you're up again at the crack of dawn" (1989, 110).

For Spike Lee, the effort was worth it. Although Paramount turned down the project, concerned about possible consequences of the riot scene, Universal underwrote the film with a $6.5 million budget, and *Do the Right Thing* catapulted Lee into the national spotlight. It also made him one of the most controversial directors of our time. Anticipating audiences everywhere, the critics disagreed over the film's intentions and effects. In particular, they disagreed about the inconclusive ending, which pairs a text by Martin Luther King denouncing violence with a text by Malcolm X justifying violence as a form of self-defense. John Simon in *The National Review* questioned Lee's integrity, arguing that an artist need not have the answers but must ask the questions honestly. "It must, even if it knows that there are no answers—and not just no easy answers—try to shed as much light as it sensitively and searchingly can. And it must be fair to all sides or be candid about which side it is taking. Above all, it must know itself." *Do the Right Thing*, concluded the reviewer, is "a clever film that . . . outsmarts itself" (Simon 1989, 46). David Denby of *New York* magazine agreed, maintaining that "the end of the movie is a shambles, and if some audiences go wild, [the director] is partly responsible" (Denby 1989, 56). In contrast, Peter Travers of *Rolling Stone* praised Lee for letting the audience think for itself. Travers saw the film as "a devastating portrait of black America pushed to the limit, with the outcome still to be written" and believed that it was "more likely to provoke debate than destruction" (1989, 29).

Whether *Do the Right Thing* generates more light or heat depends partly on the conditions under which it is viewed. Some teachers may be reluctant to screen a film so explicit in its language and controversial in its themes. But if we cannot create the right conditions in a classroom, what are the alternatives? "There is only one way to do the wrong thing about *Do the Right Thing,*" Peter Travers concluded. "That would be to ignore it."

Suggested Films and Readings

More Films by Spike Lee

> *She's Gotta Have It* (1986)
>
> *School Daze* (1988)
>
> *Mo' Better Blues* (1990)
>
> *Jungle Fever* (1991)

More Films of Special Interest

> *Hallelujah* (1929) King Vidor
>
> *Imitation of Life* (1934) John M. Stahl
>
> *Cabin in the Sky* (1943) Vincente Minnelli
>
> *Cry the Beloved Country* (1951) Alexander Korda
>
> *Carmen Jones* (1954) Otto Preminger
>
> *Blackboard Jungle* (1955) Richard Brooks
>
> *Putney Swope* (1969) Robert Downey
>
> *The Great White Hope* (1970) Martin Ritt
>
> *Cotton Comes to Harlem* (1970) Ossie Davis
>
> *A Soldier's Story* (1971) Norman Jewison
>
> *Shaft* (1971) Gordon Parks, Sr.
>
> *Sounder* (1972) Martin Ritt
>
> *Beverly Hills Cop* (1984) Martin Brest
>
> *A Dry White Season* (1990) Euzham Palcy
>
> *Boyz N the Hood* (1991) John Singleton
>
> *New Jack City* (1991) Mario Van Peebles

Books and Articles about Spike Lee and Do the Right Thing

Denby, David. "He's Gotta Have It." (Review of *Do the Right Thing*.) *New York.* 26 June 1989: 52–54.

Doherty, Thomas. 1990. "*Do the Right Thing.*" *Film Quarterly* 13: 35–40.

Lee, Spike, with Lisa Jones. 1989. *Do the Right Thing: A Spike Lee Joint.* New York: Fireside. (This companion volume to the film includes a script, selected storyboards, full credits, production notes, and Spike Lee's running journal of film ideas. Lee has published similar books for all his films.)

Nowell-Smith, Geoffrey. "*Blackass Talk: Do the Right Thing.*" *Sight and Sound.* Autumn 1989: 281.

Simon, John. "My Thing, Right or Wrong." (Review of *Do the Right Thing.*) *National Review.* 4 August 1989: 45–46, 50.

Travers, Peter. "The Right Stuff." (Review of *Do the Right Thing.*) *Rolling Stone.* 29 June 1989: 27, 29.

Books on Black Cinema

Bates, Karen Grigsby. "They've Gotta Have Us: Hollywood's Black Directors." *New York Times Magazine,* 14 July 1991: 14–44.

Bogle, Donald. [1973] 1989. *Toms, Coons, Mulattoes, Mammies, & Bucks: An Interpretive History of Blacks in American Films.* New York: Continuum.

Cripps, Thomas. 1977. *Slow Fade to Black: The Negro in American Film, 1900–1942.* New York: Oxford University Press.

Null, Gary. 1975. *Black Hollywood: The Black Performer in Motion Pictures.* New York: Citadel.

Questions for Reflection and Discussion

1. *Do the Right Thing* presents more characters than do most films. How does Spike Lee keep them all alive? How does he create a sense of community among them? To what extent is the block itself a character in the film?

2. Is the central issue between Sal and the community or does it involve other people, other groups?

3. Who are the victims of the violence in this film? Where do you think the blame lies? Does the film suggest solutions?

4. What is the function of the disk jockey, Mister Señor Love Daddy? Of Da Mayor? Of Mother Sister?

5. Spike Lee has been commended for his ability to keep up the momentum through the entire film. Do you agree? What helps to maintain the pace?

6. What motivates Mookie to throw the trash can through the window of Sal's pizzeria? At the end of the movie, does Mookie "do the right thing"? Explain.

7. Many of the characters in this film seem inarticulate. Smiley stutters. Radio Raheem speaks chiefly through his radio. Mookie accuses Tina of choking her speech with obscenities. How does this film dramatize the frustrations of expressing deeply felt emotions and beliefs?

8. What parallels can be drawn between the film and historical or current events?

9. Several conflicts are presented in the film: between Sal and Buggin' Out, between the police and the community, between the words of Martin Luther King and those of Malcolm X. Do you think the director takes sides? How can you tell?

10. What do you think has been learned by the end of the film? Who has learned the most?

Topics for Further Study

1. Spike Lee kept a journal of his ideas for this film from December 25, 1978, to August 7, 1988. His journal and production notes have been published with the script. Read them and tell how they shed light on the completed film.

2. When *Do the Right Thing* was released in 1989, it provoked a battle of critical responses. Read some of the reviews from that time, and summarize the different points of view. How do you account for such strong and varying reactions?

3. American films have featured African American actors and subjects, but, until recently, few directors of color. Investigate the history of black artists and themes in the cinema. What patterns do you find? Do you see any current trends that may break these patterns? You may want to consider these films: *The Emperor Jones* (1933), *A Raisin in the Sun* (1961), *The Great White Hope* (1970), *Shaft* (1971), *Superfly* (1972), *Beverly Hills Cop* (1984), *A Soldier's Story* (1984), *Glory* (1989), *Harlem Nights* (1989).

4. Scenes to analyze:
   • The introduction to Stuyvesant Street.
   • Mother Sister greets Da Mayor.
   • Da Mayor gets a break from Sal's Famous Pizzeria.
   • The Corner Men discuss Korean enterprise.
   • Buggin' Out confronts Sal about the Wall of Fame.
   • The racial slur sequence.
   • The johnny pump scene.
   • The music contest between Radio Raheem and the Latinos.
   • The riot.
   • Sal and Mookie part.

18 Awakenings

Directed by Penny Marshall; screenplay by Steven Zaillian; based on the book by Oliver Sacks; photography by Miroslav Ondricek; edited by Jerry Greenberg and Battle Davis; music by Randy Newman; production design by Anton Furst; released by Columbia Pictures in 1990. [121 minutes]

Leonard Loew ....*Robert De Niro*
Dr. Malcolm Sayer...................*Robin Williams*
Eleanor Costello......................*Julie Kavner*
Mrs. Loew .... *Ruth Nelson*
Dr. Kaufman ....*John Heard*
Paula ....*Penelope Ann Miller*

Soon after World War I, the world was plagued by a strange disease called "sleeping sickness." Nearly five million people were afflicted by the epidemic. Some of those who survived as children later slipped into mental states so deep that they seemed frozen alive, conscious and thoughtful yet speechless and inert, destined to sit motionless for decades like the living dead. In the late 1960s, Dr. Oliver Sacks was assigned to a hospital where eighty of these survivors had been immured for more than forty years. Dr. Sacks became intrigued by their condition and took a compassionate interest in the personalities imprisoned in their passive bodies. When he learned about L-dopa, a new miracle drug that was being used to treat Parkinson's disease, he began a campaign against the hospital's rigid administration to try the drug on his patients. His untiring efforts were rewarded. One by one, after he administered the drug, the patients awoke from their stony sleep. Some began to walk, to write, to sing, to dance. For the first time in years they were able to play cards and visit the world outside as fully human beings. But while many experienced the joy of life, others felt disoriented and depressed. Having succumbed to the disease in their youth, they had awakened as old men and women, with the best years of their lives having been stolen from them. In time, the daily dosages of L-dopa began to have unsettling effects. The patients

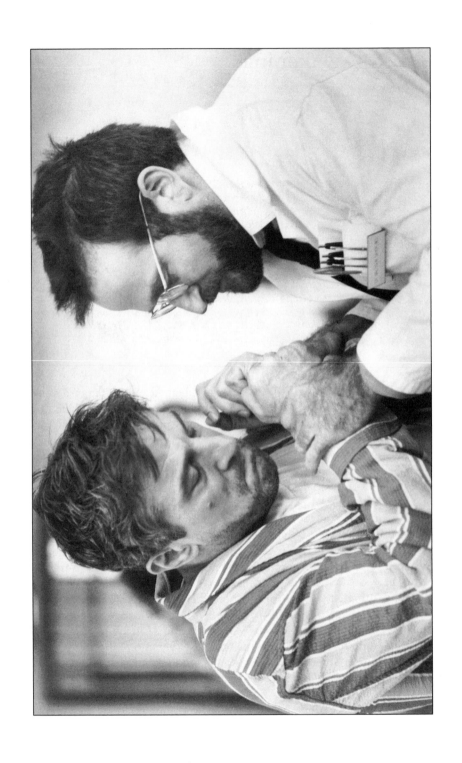

became irritable, violent, dangerous; the drug was discontinued, and they returned to their catatonic prisons. Dr. Sacks's experiment is recounted in his lucid, often eloquent work, *Awakenings*, first published in 1973 and reprinted many times as a classic study of the human face of medicine.

Penny Marshall's film tells the story in its own way. Her adaptation of Sacks's book reveals as much about the nature of filmmaking and mass entertainment as it does about the nature of a terrible disease and the people it affects. Steven Zaillian's screenplay focuses on the relationship between Dr. Malcolm Sayer (the screen counterpart of Dr. Sacks) and one patient, Leonard Loew. Robin Williams plays the doctor as a shy, brilliant researcher who is more comfortable with specimens than with human beings. Robert De Niro plays Leonard as a brilliant student of literature and life who is freed from the vault of his catatonic state, only to be locked into it again of his own volition. It is primarily the story of a friendship that induces two awakenings: Leonard's liberation from *encephalitis lethargica* and Dr. Sayer's release from a lifetime of timidity.

It is also a double love story. Leonard, who has not experienced erotic love in more than forty years, develops a lively affection for Paula (Penelope Ann Miller), a young woman who comes to visit her father at the ward. Meanwhile, Dr. Sayer begins to recognize his feelings for Eleanor Costello (Julie Kavner) the nurse who supports his arduous struggle against an insensitive hospital establishment. Throughout the film, though mainly in the background, a cast of patients and hospital employees sets off the central roles with vignettes that are alternately comic, touching, and antagonistic.

The principal performances are remarkable. Audiences familiar with Robin Williams's frenetic humor in his early television series, *Mork and Mindy*, or in recent films like *Good Morning, Vietnam* (1987) and *Dead Poets Society* (1989), may be surprised by his understated portrayal of Dr. Sayer. Williams is said to have prepared for the role by visiting various institutions and by observing Oliver Sacks with patients at Mount Carmel Hospital in New York (Elder 1991, 94). De Niro's acting marks a similar departure from earlier roles. In contrast to his violent, city-hardened characters in *The Godfather Part II* (1974), *Raging Bull* (1980), and *Goodfellas* (1990), De Niro's Leonard is boyish, thoughtful, and genteel. Much of the credit for these unusual performances is due to the director.

Penny Marshall was born in the Bronx, New York, in 1942. The child of a filmmaker (Tony Marshall) and a dance coach (Marjorie Marshall), she was at home in the entertainment world from an early age, appearing in the Ted Mack Amateur Hour and the Jackie Gleason Show. Beginning in 1977, she starred as Laverne in the popular *Laverne and Shirley* television sitcom. She also acted in several motion pictures (*The Savage Seven* and *How Sweet It Is!*, 1968; *How Come Nobody's On Our Side?*, 1975) before directing her first film, *Jumpin' Jack Flash*, in 1986. Her next film, *Big*, was a big hit—Cunnett calls it the most successful feature ever directed by a woman (1988, 52). Does it make a difference that *Awakenings* was directed by a woman? The issues of sexual politics in Hollywood have been taken up by critics like Barbara Quart. Quart makes a distinction between mainstream movies, like *Big*, and independent films, like *Hester Street* (Joan Micklin Silver, 1975). She asks what it means to be a woman making movies, and she examines the styles and subjects of the women who have made them, from Dorothy Arzner in the 1930s to Joan Micklin Silver in the 1980s.

The reception to *Awakenings* has varied. Some reviewers criticized Marshall for treating the subject too lightly, calling it an "upscale heart tugger" (Corliss 1990, 53), "a volatile mix of strength and weakness, intellectual boldness and commercial calculation" (Denby 1990, 77), and "a fairy tale forged uneasily out of facts [which] both sentimentalizes its story and oversimplifies it beyond recognition" (Maslin 1990, C11). Other critics appreciated the gentle warmth and humor that Marshall brings to an otherwise unpalatable subject, stressing the human side of human disability for viewers who might not otherwise look beyond the dismaying symptoms that separate the afflicted from themselves (Elder 1991, 94; Johnson 1990, 52).

Filmmakers have looked at illnesses and handicaps before. There is a relatively underpopulated but persistent genre of films about individuals who are set apart by disabilities and about the individuals who try to help them. They range from *Dr. Ehrlich's Magic Bullet* (1940) and *The Miracle Worker* (1962) to *The Elephant Man* (1980), *Rain Man* (1988), and *My Left Foot* (1989). Many of these films are based on actual case histories. The book by Oliver Sacks documents the histories of twenty patients whose lives were frozen in Mount Carmel Hospital when he arrived. In a style that is both expressive and medically precise, Dr. Sacks strives "to picture a world, a variety of worlds—the landscapes of being in which these patients reside" (1987, xx).

Sacks's book is a self-consciously literary work. Its title comes from Ibsen's *When We Dead Awaken*. There are references throughout to John Donne, Rainer Maria Rilke, D. H. Lawrence, Ludwig von Wittgenstein, and W. H. Auden, who visited the hospital and saw poetic and religious implications in the disease. For Auden, "awakening was an awakening above all to the *responsibilities* of being human, after decades of being cut off from these in a sleep both psychological and allegorical" (Sacks 1987, xxviii). For Sacks, the awakening was also to one's own humanity, since "other worlds, other lives, even though so different from our own, have the power of arousing the sympathetic imagination, of awakening an intense and often creative resonance in others" (1987, xxx).

All of us, to some degree, have slipped into our own lethargies, have lost touch with the fullness of life, with the vitality of other human beings. Through the miracle of L-dopa, Sacks's patients could once again appreciate the ordinary things—the joy of music, friendships, a beautiful day—with an exhilaration that is often lost with childhood. Yet this miracle was temporary. In the movie, Leonard lapses into fits of paranoia and megalomania that intensify until the drug is stopped. The real Leonard experienced even more violent episodes of libidinous rages, sexual hallucinations, and grandiosity (Sacks 1987, 188–201). Sacks calls this period "tribulation," likening it to the day of doom in Wycliffe's Bible and to the turmoil before one faces death. He goes on to describe a final phase, "accommodation," when the patient accepts what is inevitable. In a moment of lucidity, Leonard realized that the miracle had failed: "Now I accept the whole situation. It was wonderful, terrible, dramatic and comic. It is finally *sad*, and that's all there is to it. I'm best left alone—no more drugs" (1987, 201). The doses were stopped. Leonard slipped back into his coma and eventually to death. "I am a living candle," he had written. "I am consumed that you may learn. New things will be seen in the light of my suffering" (Elder 1991, 95).

Suggested Films and Readings

Films by Penny Marshall

> *Jumpin' Jack Flash* (1986)
>
> *Big* (1988)

More Films Directed by Women

> Dorothy Arzner: *Christopher Strong* (1933), *Nana* (1934), *Craig's Wife* (1936), *Dance, Girl, Dance* (1940)
>
> Joyce Chopra: *Smooth Talk* (1985). [Based on the story, "Where Are You Going, Where Have You Been?" by Joyce Carol Oates.]

Diane Kurys, France: *Peppermint Soda* (1977), *Entre Nous* (1983)

Ida Lupino: *Outrage* (1950), *Hard, Fast, and Beautiful* (1951), *The Bigamist* (1953)

Elaine May: *A New Leaf* (1971), *The Heartbreak Kid* (1972), *Mikey and Nicky* (1976)

Mira Nair, India: *Salaam Bombay!* (1988)

Euzhan Palcy, USA: *A Dry White Season* (1989)

Pat Rozema, Canada: *I've Heard the Mermaids Singing* (1987)

Susan Seidelman: *Smithereens* (1982), *Desperately Seeking Susan* (1985), *Making Mr. Right* (1987)

Joan Micklin Silver: *Hester Street* (1975), *Chilly Scenes of Winter* (1979), *Crossing Delancey* (1988)

Margarethe von Trotta, Germany: *The Lost Honor of Katarina Blum* (1977), *Marianne and Juliane* (1981)

Agnès Varda, France: *Cleo From 5 to 7* (1961), *Le Bonheur* (1965), *One Sings, the Other Doesn't* (1977)

Claudia Weill: *Girlfriends* (1978), *It's My Turn* (1980)

Lina Wertmuller, Italy: *The Seduction of Mimi* (1972), *Swept Away* (1974), *Seven Beauties* (1975)

Film Reviews of Awakenings

Ansen, David. *Newsweek*. 24 Dec. 1990: 62.

Corliss, Richard. "Schemes and Dreams for Christmas." *Time*. 24 Dec. 1990: 77–80.

Cunneff, Tom, with Jack Kelley. "Penny Marshall Finally Leaves *Laverne* Behind and Scores *Big* as a Director—So Why the Long Face?" *People Weekly*. 15 Aug. 1988: 52–54.

Denby, David. "The Good Doctor." *New York*. 17 Dec. 1990: 68, 71.

Elder, Sean. "Movies." *Vogue*. Jan. 1991: 94–95, 98.

Johnson, Brian. "Hollywood Heavyweights: A Black Christmas from Hollywood." *Maclean's* 103: 52. 48–50.

Klawans, Stuart. "Holiday Celluloid Wrap-Up." *The Nation*. 7-14 Jan. 1991: 22–24.

Maslin, Janet. *The New York Times*. 20 Jan. 1990: C11.

Travers, Peter. "Awakenings." *The New York Times*. 20 Dec. 1990: C11, C18.

Books of Special Interest

Quart, Barbara Koenig. 1988. *Women Directors: The Emergence of a New Cinema.* New York: Praeger.

This is a good introductory survey of women who have directed films in the United States, in Western and Eastern Europe, and in the Third World. Keonig includes both mainstream and independent filmmakers, emphasizing the broad range of talents, visions, and accomplishments among these directors.

Sacks, Oliver. *Awakenings.* 1987. New York: Dutton.

Written by the talented neurologist and humanist whose work inspired Penny Marshall's film, this book presents the case histories of twenty patients at Mount Carmel hospital who were roused from decades of "sleeping sickness" through Sacks's experiments with the miracle drug L-dopa.

Books about Women and Film

DeLauretus, Teresa. 1984. *Alice Doesn't: Feminism, Semiotics, Cinema.* Bloomington: Indiana University Press.

Haskell, Molly. 1974. *From Reverence to Rape: The Treatment of Women in the Movies.* New York: Holt, Rinehart, Winston.

Kaplan, E. Ann. 1983. *Women and Film: Both Sides of the Camera.* New York: Methuen.

Kuhn, Annette. 1982. *Women's Pictures: Feminism and Cinema.* London: Routledge & Kegan Paul.

Kay, Karyn and Gerald Peary, eds. 1977. *Women and the Cinema: A Critical Anthology.* New York: Dutton.

Rosen, Marjorie. 1973. *Popcorn Venus: Women, Movies and the American Dream.* New York: Avon.

Questions for Discussion

1. *Awakenings* deals with a serious illness, *encephalitis lethargica,* which affected millions of lives in the first half of this century. How common are films about handicaps and diseases today? Why? How does Penny Marshall's film treat the subject of this illness?

2. Several plots are intertwined in the film. First, there is the central relationship between a doctor and his patient. Second, there are

two love stories: between a doctor and a nurse and between a patient and a visitor. Third, there is a conflict between a crusading doctor and a resistant hospital establishment. How well are these plots combined? Do you see any others?

3. The chief roles are played by two accomplished actors: Robin Williams and Robert De Niro. What special qualities do they bring to these roles? Does your knowledge of their work as actors contribute to or interfere with your appreciation of this film? Given Penny Marshall's talents and her film and television experience, how do you think her directing may have affected these performances?

4. *Awakenings* features a large supporting cast of patients, visitors, and hospital employees. Which of these secondary roles seem most memorable? What do they contribute to the film?

5. Although most of the story is set during the late 1960s, it is introduced by a scene from Leonard's childhood. What is the effect of this visit to an earlier era? How aware are you, throughout the film, of the historical setting? What makes you aware that it takes place in the sixties?

6. The title *Awakenings* could be applied to several people in the film, both patients and doctors, as well as to the audience itself. In what sense do these individuals or groups "awaken"? In what sense were they asleep?

Topics for Further Study

1. The film *Awakenings* was based on a book of the same name by Dr. Oliver Sacks, who first visited the wards of New York's Mount Carmel Hospital in the late 1960s and began working with patients who had been suffering from "sleeping sickness" for more than forty years. Read the book to discover how much of the film is true.

2. Find out more about *encephalitis lethargica*, the medical term for "sleeping sickness," and the epidemic which afflicted five million people worldwide in the 1920s.

3. A number of movies have focused on the human drama of an individual who seeks to help someone afflicted with a disability, including *The Miracle Worker, The Elephant Man, Rain Man,* and *My Left Foot.* How many others can you think of? What are the

attractions and risks of telling these stories through a medium of mass entertainment?

4. The critical response to *Awakenings* was split between those who thought it was a genuinely moving film experience and those who saw it as an exploitation film. Read a sampling of the reviews from December, 1990, and January, 1991. Summarize the major viewpoints, and explain which views you find most convincing.

5. Scenes to analyze:

   • The opening episode from Leonard's childhood.
   • Dr. Sayer arrives at the hospital.
   • Lucy drops her glasses.
   • Dr. Sayer awakens to find Leonard missing from his bed.
   • The nurses' soap opera is interrupted by real life.
   • Dr. Sayer makes a plea for funds to buy L-dopa.
   • Leonard's mother reacts to his cure.
   • Leonard and Sayer bid farewell to each other.

Appendix 1:
More Great Films

There are many ways to organize a film unit or a course. Film adaptations can be matched with the literature on which they're based. Films can also be grouped thematically, like other works. They can be studied by director, genre, period, or nationality. What follows are a few suggested titles arranged to illustrate some popular options.

Film and Literature

Wuthering Heights (1939) William Wyler

Pride and Prejudice (1940) Robert Z. Leonard

Oliver Twist (1948) David Lean

The Old Man and the Sea (1958) John Sturges

The Innocents (1961) Jack Clayton (an adaptation of *The Turn of the Screw*)

To Kill a Mockingbird (1962) Robert Mulligan

Billy Budd (1962) Peter Ustinov

One Flew Over the Cuckoo's Nest (1975) Miloš Forman

A Passage to India (1984) David Lean

Leading Themes

Growing Up

Oliver Twist (1948) David Lean

Rebel Without a Cause (1955) Nicholas Ray

Lord of the Flies (1963) Peter Brook

The Graduate (1967) Mike Nichols

Stand by Me (1986) Rob Reiner

The Black Experience

A Raisin in the Sun (1961) Daniel Petrie

The Learning Tree (1969) Gordon Parks

A *Soldier's Story* (1984) Norman Jewison
Glory (1989) Edward Zwick
Do the Right Thing (1989) Spike Lee

Overcoming Handicaps

The Miracle Worker (1962) Arthur Penn
The Elephant Man (1980) David Lynch
My Left Foot (1989) Jim Sheridan

School Days

The Blackboard Jungle (1955) Richard Brooks
Rebel Without a Cause (1955) Nicholas Ray
The Breakfast Club (1985) John Hughes
Stand and Deliver (1987) Ramon Menendez
School Daze (1988) Spike Lee
Dead Poets Society (1989) Peter Weir

Nature versus the Human Race

King Kong (1933) Merian C. Cooper and Ernest B. Schoedsack
Moby Dick (1956) John Huston
The Birds (1963) Alfred Hitchcock

The World Looks at War

All Quiet on the Western Front (1930) Lewis Milestone, USA
Grand Illusion (1937) Jean Renoir, France
The Best Years of Our Lives (1946) William Wyler, USA
The Ballad of a Soldier (1959) Grigori Chukhrai, USSR
Yojimbo (1961) Akira Kurosawa, Japan
Dr. Strangelove or: How I Learned to Stop Worrying and Love the Bomb (1964) Stanley Kubrick, England
Das Boot (1981) Wolfgang Petersen, Germany

Genres

Science Fiction

Things to Come (1936) William Cameron Menzies
Forbidden Planet (1956) Fred McLeod Wilcox

Invasion of the Body Snatchers (1956) Don Siegel

Fantastic Voyage (1966) Richard Fleischer

Close Encounters of the Third Kind (1977) Steven Spielberg

Screwball Comedy

It Happened One Night (1934) Frank Capra

My Man Godfrey (1936) Gregory La Cava

Bringing Up Baby (1938) Howard Hawks

Mr. Smith Goes to Washington (1939) Frank Capra

His Girl Friday (1940) Howard Hawks

Mystery

The Maltese Falcon (1941) John Huston

Double Indemnity (1944) Billy Wilder

The Killers (1946) Robert Siodmak

Touch of Evil (1958) Orson Welles

Chinatown (1974) Roman Polanski

The Musical

Forty-Second Street (1933) Lloyd Bacon

Swing Time (1936) George Stevens

Singin' in the Rain (1952) Gene Kelly, Stanley Donen

West Side Story (1961) Robert Wise

Oliver! (1968) Carol Reed

Tommy (1975) Ken Russell

Appendix 2:
Four Film Projects

The following four projects, all taken from community college film courses, are examples of what students can do to supplement class screenings and discussions.

1. Oral Presentation

This is an opportunity to study one film in some detail and share what you learn with others in the class. You are encouraged to work in groups of two or three for each presentation. Each group selects a film from the course listing (films that we will be screening later in the term) and prepares a brief introduction, handouts, and questions for discussion.

The introduction will be oral. It may include background information about the film's origins, its creators and cast, its reception, its main themes. You may also want to point out particular things to look for in the film. Please limit your remarks to ten minutes or less.

The handouts should include film credits (director, scriptwriter, the principal actors, etc.), further readings (books, articles, reviews), and study questions. Please bring enough copies for everyone.

Using your study questions as a guide, lead a class discussion after viewing the film. You may want to focus on the acting, directing, film techniques, or theme. You may explore the class's emotional responses or examine the film's symbolic levels.

Note: You will be graded as a group, so full group cooperation is a must. Be sure that you select people you can work with.

2. Behind the Scenes

We often appreciate a movie more when we know how it was made. What went into its creation behind the scenes? For example, how did the art director design the sets for *Citizen Kane*? How did the photographer achieve those striking camera movements and lighting effects?

Where did the ideas for the screenplay come from, and what did each writer contribute to the script?

This assignment is an opportunity to look behind the scenes at a particular aspect of filmmaking which interests you. First, select a film you would like to learn more about. Then, choose one of the following topics and write a report on what you learn.

A. *Script Writing.* Who was responsible for the film script? Where did the main idea originate? If the film is based on literature, read the original text and compare it to the final film.

B. *Photography.* Who was the film's chief cinematographer? What is he or she most noted for? Are there any technical innovations in camera work or lighting? How were they achieved?

C. *Set Design.* Who was involved in selecting and creating the film's sets? Were any special problems encountered in making the sets? How were they solved? How important are the sets in the final film?

D. *Music.* Does the film use familiar music or an original score? What musical decisions were made by the composer? What effects was the composer striving for? Are different melodies used for different characters or scenes? How do they contribute to the total film experience?

F. *Direction.* Some directors have a stronger hand than others in the making of a film. Directors may be interested in different elements of filmmaking. What role did the director have in producing the film you chose? What are the director's hallmarks in this and other films?

E. *Acting.* Select one or more actors in the film and find out more about them. Why do you think they were chosen for the film? What other roles have they played? Are they versatile or stereotyped? What can you learn about their behavior on or off the set during the film's production?

F. *Reception.* Do some research to find out how the film was received during its first release. What did the critics say? How did the general public respond? How do you account for the reception in its own time and today?

3. Shot-by-Shot Analysis

Good movies, like good stories, poems, and plays, are best read more than once. Under close analysis, a well-made film can reveal qualities and meanings which we miss the first time through. The purpose of this assignment is to take another, careful look at part of a familiar film in order to appreciate how it was made and how it works.

A. Select a film to study from the course list. View the entire film, then choose a scene (from ten to twenty shots in length) to analyze.

B. Do a shot-by-shot analysis of the scene. Your analysis should include the following for each shot:

1. A brief description of the shot (action, setting, characters)

2. Framing (close-up, medium shot, long shot)

3. Camera angles (low angle, high angle, eye level)

4. Camera movement (tilt, crane, zoom, pan, tracking, none)

5. Lighting (high key, low key, back lighting, front lighting, normal)

6. Sound (describe any dialogue, music, voice over, or sound effects)

7. Transitions (cut, dissolve, wipe, other optical effects)

Note: You may list the elements (1–7) for each shot or describe them in paragraph form, but they should all be accounted for.

C. Answer the following questions about your chosen scene:

1. *Plot.* How does this scene contribute to the ongoing story? Give a brief overview of your chosen film (what is it about?) and tell how the scene fits in.

2. *Point of view.* Does this scene present an objective view of events, or does it represent someone's subjective account? Explain. How is the camera used to emphasize this point of view?

3. *Character.* What does this scene tell you about the major character or characters? Refer as specifically as you can to the actors' movements, words, and dress as revealed by the camera.

4. *Tone.* Describe the overall mood of this scene. Is it mysterious, funny, sad? How do the lighting and camera work help to create this mood?

Note: You are encouraged to complete the shot-by-shot analysis in groups of two. Students have found that collaborative viewing helps them to see more clearly (four eyes are better than two) and to think more sharply (discussion nourishes ideas) than they would alone. You are expected to answer the questions in part three by yourself.

4. Fiction into Film

Most movies these days seem to be based on books. Literary classics are revived for the modern screen, bestsellers are converted into box-office sales, and even obscure stories become major motion pictures. This is your chance to adapt a work of written fiction into film. In the process, you'll learn what goes into the making of a movie, you'll appreciate the differences between two important media, and you'll become a better reader of both fiction and film.

Begin by reading lots of fiction: short stories, novels, and narrative poems which might lend themselves to adaptation. Your job is to find a promising story and explain its cinematic possibilities to the others in your group. This may be done in a written *film proposal* that outlines the plot, sketches the main characters, suggests locations for the major scenes, and speculates on the technical challenges that a camera crew might face.

Reread the original story closely with the film in mind. Look for details of character to help you *cast the principal actors.* Pay attention to the setting so you can *scout locations* and *design interior sets.* You'll need to be aware of the story's point of view in order to decide on *camera setups* for each shot. Most important, you'll need to understand the story's tone and theme if your film is going to be faithful to the original.

Once the group has decided on a story, the film proposal can be transformed into a storyboard or shooting script. A *storyboard* tells the story, shot by shot, in pictures and text. The pictures show what the camera will see. The text gives the dialogue and action; it also gives cues about camera position, lighting, editing, and other production technicalities. A *shooting script* also describes each shot, but without pictures. Like the storyboard, the shooting script is a blueprint for constructing the final film.

In addition to the *actors* and *script writers*, your group will need production specialists, including: a *director* to direct the action and overall shooting of each scene; a *script supervisor* to plan each day of shooting and check the results against the storyboard or shooting script; a *cinematographer* to set up and operate the camera; a *set designer* to create the sets or furnish them with props; a *lighting crew* to illuminate each indoor scene, a *sound technician* in charge of the sound track (sound effects, music, dialogue), and an *editor* to splice together the final film, or combine the final video electronically if you use videotape.

A successful film production depends on many things, not the least of which is responsible group participation. Every member of the group has a specific job to do. The group depends on everyone doing her or his job reliably. Only if everybody works together can a work of fiction come alive on film.

Bibliography

Arnheim, Rudolph. 1969. *Art and Visual Perception: A Psychology of the Creative Eye*. Berkeley: University of California Press.

———. 1966. *Film as Art*. Berkeley: University of California Press.

Amelio, Ralph J. 1971. *Film in the Classroom: Why to Use It, How to Use It*. Dayton, Ohio: Pflaum/Standard Publishing.

Andrew, J. Dudley. 1984. *Concepts in Film Theory*. New York: Oxford University Press.

———. 1976. *The Major Film Theories: An Introduction*. New York: Oxford University Press.

Balachoff, Dimitri. 1989. "The Psychophysiology of Film and Video." *The Perfect Vision* 2:5, 50–55.

Balázs, Béla. 1970. *Theory of the Film*. New York: Dover.

Bates, Karen Grigsby. 1991. "They've Gotta Have Us: Hollywood's Black Directors." *New York Times Magazine*, 14 July: 14–44.

Bazin, André. *What Is Cinema?* [1958–63] 1967. Berkeley: University of California Press. (1967 edition translated by Hugh Gray.)

Beach, Richard. 1979. "Issues of Censorship and Research on Effects of and Response to Reading." In James E. Davis, ed, *Dealing with Censorship*. Urbana, Ill.: NCTE. 131–153.

Beja, Morris. 1979a. *Film & Literature: An Introduction*. New York: Longman.

———. 1979b. "The Grapes of Wrath." In Morris Beja, ed., *Film & Literature: An Introduction*. New York: Longman. 107–117.

Benjamin, Walter. [1935] 1985. "The Work of Art in the Age of Mechanical Reproduction." Reprinted in Gerald Mast and Marshall Cohen, eds., *Film Theory and Criticism: Introductory Readings*. 3rd edition. New York: Oxford University Press. 675–694.

———. *Illuminations*. 1968. Edited with an introduction by Hannah Arendt. New York: Harcourt Brace.

Bluestone, George. 1957a. *Novels into Film*. Baltimore: Johns Hopkins Press.

———. 1957b. "The Grapes of Wrath." In George Bluestone, ed., *Novels into Film*. Baltimore: Johns Hopkins Press. 147–69.

Bogle, Donald. [1973] 1989. *Toms, Coons, Mulattoes, Mammies, & Bucks: An Interpretive History of Blacks in American Films*. New York: Continuum.

Bohnenkamp, Dennis R., and Sam L. Grogg, eds. 1978. *The American Film Institute Guide to College Courses in Film and Television*. Princeton, N.J.: Peterson's Guides for the American Film Institute.

Bordwell, David, and Kristin Thompson. 1986. *Film as Art: An Introduction.* New York: Knopf.

Boyum, Joy Gould. 1985. *Double Exposure: Fiction Into Film.* New York: New American Library.

Brunette, Peter, and David Wills. 1989. *Screen/Play: Derrida and Film Theory.* Princeton, N.J.: Princeton University Press.

Burress, Lee. 1979. "A Brief Report of the 1977 NCTE Censorship Survey." *Dealing With Censorship.* Ed. James E. Davis. Urbana, Ill: NCTE. 14–47.

Canby, Vincent. 1989. "Classics Thrive on Screen Tests." *The New York Times,* 10 September, Section 2: 19+.

———. 1984. "Film View: Third World Truths from *Sugar Cane Alley.*" *The New York Times,* 2 April: C15.

Capra, Frank. 1971. *The Name Above the Title: An Autobiography.* New York: Macmillan.

Carringer, Robert L. 1985. *The Making of* Citizen Kane. Berkeley: University of California Press.

Chatman, Seymour. 1978. *Story and Discourse: Narrative Structure in Fiction and Film.* Ithaca, N.Y.: Cornell University Press.

Ciment, Michel. 1974. *Kazan on Kazan.* New York: Viking.

Cohen, Keith. 1979. *Film and Fiction: The Dynamics of Exchange.* New Haven, Conn.: Yale University Press.

Comden, Betty, and Adolph Green. 1972. *Singin' in the Rain.* New York: Viking.

Congress of the United States, Office of Technology Assessment. *Copyright & Home Copying: Technology Challenges the Law.* OTA- CIT-422. Washington, DC: U.S. Government Printing Office, October 1989.

Cook, David A. 1981. *A History of Narrative Film.* New York: Norton.

Corliss, Richard. 1990. "Schemes and Dreams for Christmas." 24 December: 77.

Costanzo, William V. 1984. *Double Exposure: Composing through Writing and Film.* Upper Montclair, N.J.: Boynton/Cook.

———. 1985. "Fiction into Film: Learning Literature with a Movie Camera." *Teaching English in the Two-Year College.* 52–56.

———, ed. 1987. *Report by the NCTE Committee on Film Study in American Schools.* ERIC Documentation No. ED 287 165.

Cowie, Peter. 1973. *A Ribbon of Dreams: The Cinema of Orson Welles.* New York: A. S. Barnes.

Cripps, Thomas. 1977. *Slow Fade to Black: The Negro in American Film, 1900–1942.* New York: Oxford University Press.

Cunneff, Tom, with Jack Kelley. 1988. "Penny Marshall Finally Leaves *Laverne* Behind and Scores *Big* as a Director—So Why the Long Face?" *People Weekly.* 15 August: 52–54.

Davis, James E., ed. 1979. *Dealing with Censorship.* Urbana, Ill.: NCTE.

De Stefano, George. 1984. *Cinèaste* 23: 4–45.

Denby, David. 1990. "The Good Doctor." *New York,* 15 August: 53–54.

———. 1989. "He's Gotta Have It." *New York,* 26 June: 52–54.

Dick, Bernard F. 1978. *Anatomy of Film.* New York: St. Martin's Press.

Doherty, Thomas. 1989. "Do The Right Thing." *Film Quarterly* 13: 35–40.

Donelson, Kenneth L. 1979. "Censorship in the 1970s: Some Ways to Handle It When It Comes." In James E. Davis, ed., *Dealing With Censorship.* Urbana, Ill.: NCTE. 162–179.

———. 1973. "The Censorship of Non-Print Media Comes to the English Classroom." *English Journal* 62: 1226–1227.

Draigh, David. 1988. *Behind the Screen: The American Museum of the Moving Image Guide to Who Does What in Motion Pictures and Television.* New York: Abbeville Press.

Deutelbaum, Marshall, and Leland Poague, eds. 1986. *A Hitchcock Reader.* Ames: Iowa University Press.

Eisenstein, Sergei M. 1949. *Film Form: Essays in Film Theory.* Edited and translated by Jay Leyda. New York: Harcourt, Brace & World.

Elder, Sean. 1991. "Movies." *Vogue,* January: 94–95.

———. 1942. *The Film Sense.* Edited and translated by Jay Leyda. New York: Harcourt, Brace & World.

Fantel, Hans. 1990a. "Film to Videotape: A Ticklish Transfer." *The New York Times,* 25 March, 2: 18, 32.

———. 1990b. "HDTV, Videodisks and Sharper Images Come to the Fore." *The New York Times,* 30 December, 2: 24.

Fell, John L. 1975. *Film: An Introduction.* New York: Praeger.

———. 1979. *A History of Films.* New York: Holt, Rinehart and Winston.

"Film Study in English Classes." 1986. Unpublished survey. Champaign, Ill.: NCTE Committee on Film Study and the English Language Arts.

Forsdale, Joan Rosengren, and Louis Forsdale. 1966. "Film Literacy." *Teachers College Record* 67: 608–17.

French, Warren. 1973. *Filmguide to* The Grapes of Wrath. Bloomington: Indiana University Press.

Geduld, Harry M., and Ronald Gottesman. 1973. *An Illustrated Glossary of Film Terms.* New York: Holt, Rinehart and Winston.

Giannetti, Louis. 1990. *Understanding Movies.* 5th Edition. Englewood Cliffs, N.J.: Prentice Hall.

Glatzer, Richard, and John Raeburn, eds. 1975. *Frank Capra: The Man and His Films.* Ann Arbor: University of Michigan Press.

Gledhill, Christine. 1985. "Recent Developments in Feminist Criticism." In Gerald Mast and Marshall Cohen, eds., *Film Theory and Criticism: Introductory Readings.* 3rd Edition. New York: Oxford University Press.

Gottesman, Ronald, ed. 1976. *Focus on Orson Welles.* Englewood Cliffs, N.J.: Prentice-Hall.

Grant, Barry Keith, ed. 1983. *Film Study in the Undergraduate Curriculum.* New York: Modern Language Association.

Harrington, John. 1977. *Film and/as Literature.* Englewood Cliffs, N.J.: Prentice-Hall.

———. *The Rhetoric of Film.* 1973. New York: Holt, Rinehart and Winston.

Hawkes, Terence. 1977. *Structuralism & Semiotics.* London: Methuen.

Hogan, Robert F. 1979. "Some Thoughts on Censorship in the Schools." In James Davis, ed., *Dealing With Censorship*. Urbana, Ill.: NCTE. 86–95.

Horton, Andrew, and Joan Magretta, eds. 1981. *Modern European Filmmakers and the Art of Adaptation*. New York: Ungar. (Essays on more than twenty European films since World War II that have been based on literary works.)

Howlett, John. 1975. *James Dean: A Biography*. New York: Simon & Schuster.

Jenkinson, Edward B. 1979. "Dirty Dictionaries, Obscene Nursery Rhymes, and Burned Books." In James Davis, ed., *Dealing With Censorship*. Urbana, Ill.: NCTE. 2–13.

Johnson, Brian. 1990. "Hollywood Heavyweights: A Black Christmas from Hollywood." *Maclean's*. 103: 52. 48–50.

Kael, Pauline. 1971. *The Citizen Kane Book*. Boston: Little, Brown.

———. 1970. *Going Steady*. Boston: Little, Brown.

Kauffmann, Stanley. 1971. "*The Graduate*." In Stanley Kauffmann, ed., *Figures of Light: Film Criticism and Comment*. New York: Harper & Row.

Kawin, Bruce F. 1987. *How Movies Work*. New York: Macmillan.

———. 1977. *Faulkner and Film*. New York: Ungar.

———. 1982. *Faulkner's MGM Screenplays*. Knoxville: University of Tennessee Press.

Kracauer, Siegfried. 1959. *From Caligari to Hitler: A Psychological History of German Film*. New York: Noonday.

———. 1960. *Theory of Film: The Redemption of Physical Reality*. New York: Oxford University Press.

Kreidl, John Francis. 1977. *Nicholas Ray*. Boston: Twayne.

Lee, Spike, with Lisa Jones. 1989. *Do the Right Thing: A Spike Lee Joint*. New York: Fireside.

Lindsay, Vachel. 1922. *The Art of the Moving Picture*. Revised edition. New York: Macmillan.

Lynch, Joan Driscoll. 1983. *Film Education in Secondary Schools: A Study of Film Use and Teaching in Selected English and Film Courses*. New York: Garland.

Maland, Charles J. 1980. *Frank Capra*. Boston: Twayne.

Marcus, Fred, comp. 1971. *Film and Literature: Contrasts in Media*. Scranton, Pa.: Chandler.

Maslin, Janet. 1990. Review of *Awakenings*. *The New York Times*, 20 Jan: C11.

Mast, Gerald. 1981. *A Short History of the Movies*. 3rd edition. Indianapolis: Bobbs-Merrill Educational.

Mast, Gerald, and Marshall Cohen, eds. 1985. *Film Theory and Criticism: Introductory Readings*. 3rd edition. New York: Oxford University Press.

McBride, Joseph. 1977. *Orson Welles, Actor and Director*. New York: Harvest/ HBJ Books.

McDougal, Stuart Y. 1985. *Made into Movies: From Literature to Film*. New York: Holt, Rinehart and Winston.

Metz, Christian. 1974. *Film Language: A Semiotics of the Cinema*. Translated by Michael Taylor. New York: Oxford University Press.

———. 1982. *The Imaginary Signifier: Psychoanalysis and the Cinema.* Translated by Celia Britton et al. Bloomington: Indiana University Press.

Miller, Jerome K. 1979. *Applying the New Copyright Law: A Guide for Educators and Librarians.* Chicago: American Library Association.

Monaco, James. 1977. *How to Read a Film: The Art, Technology, Language, History, and Theory of Film and Media.* New York: Oxford University Press.

Mulvey, Laura. 1985. "Visual Pleasure and Narrative Cinema." In Gerald Mast and Marshall Cohen, eds., *Film Theory and Criticism: Introductory Readings.* 3rd edition. New York: Oxford University Press. 803–16.

Münsterberg, Hugo. [1916] 1970. *The Film: A Psychological Study: The Silent Photoplay in 1916.* New York: Dover.

NCTE Commission on Media. 1983. "Rationale for Integrating Media into English and the Language Arts." Urbana, Ill.: NCTE.

Nichols, Bill. 1981. *Ideology and the Image: Social Representation in the Cinema and Other Media.* Bloomington: Indiana University Press.

———, ed. 1976. *Movies and Methods: An Anthology.* Berkeley: University of California Press.

Nichols, Peter. 1990. "Movie Rentals Fade." *The New York Times.* 6 May, 2: 1+.

Norris, Christopher. 1982. *Deconstruction: Theory and Practice.* New York: Methuen.

Null, Gary. 1975. *Black Hollywood: The Black Performer in Motion Pictures.* New York: Citadel.

Peirce, Charles Sanders. 1955. *Philosophical Writings of Peirce.* Edited by Justus Buchler. New York: Dover.

Phillips, William H. 1985. *Analyzing Films: A Practical Guide.* New York: Holt, Rinehart and Winston.

Pryluck, Calvin, and Paul T. M. Hemenway. 1980. *The American Film Institute: Second Survey of Higher Education.* Los Angeles: American Film Institute.

Pudovkin, V[sevolod] I. 1960. *Film Technique [1926] and Film Acting [1935].* Edited and translated by Ivor Montagu. New York: Grove.

Quart, Barbara Koenig. 1988. *Women Directors: The Emergence of a New Cinema.* New York: Praeger.

Rosen, Philip, ed. 1986. *Narrative, Apparatus, Ideology: A Film Theory Reader.* New York: Columbia University Press.

Sacks, Oliver. 1987. *Awakenings.* New York: Dutton.

Sarris, Andrew. 1984. "Oscar Hangover, Third-World Crossover." *The Village Voice,* 24 April: 49–50.

———. 1968. *The American Cinema: Directors and Directions, 1929–1968.* New York: Dutton.

Schatz, Thomas. 1981. *Hollywood Genres: Formulas, Filmmaking, and the Studio System.* Philadelphia, Pa.: Temple University Press.

Schillaci, Anthony, and John M. Culkin, eds. 1970. *Films Deliver: Teaching Creatively With Film.* New York: Citation Press.

Scholes, Robert. 1982. *Semiotics and Interpretation.* New Haven: Yale University Press.

Schulberg, Budd. 1980. On the Waterfront: *The Final Shooting Script.* Hollywood: Samuel French.

———. 1955. *Waterfront.* New York: Random House.

Schuth, H. Wayne. 1978. *Mike Nichols.* Boston: Twayne.

Sheridan, Marion C., with Harold H. Owen, Jr., Ken Macrorie, and Fred Marcus, for NCTE. 1965. *The Motion Picture and the Teaching of English.* New York: Appleton-Century-Crofts.

Simon, John. 1989. "My Thing, Right or Wrong." *National Review.* August 4: 45–46, 50.

Sinofsky, Esther R. *Off-Air Videotaping in Education: Copyright Issues, Decision, Implications.* 1984. New York: R. R. Bowker.

Small, Robert. 1979. "Censorship and English: Some Things We Don't Seem to Think About (but Should)." In James Davis, *Dealing With Censorship.* Urbana, Ill.: 54–62.

Spoto, Donald. 1983. *The Dark Side of Genius: The Life of Alfred Hitchcock.* Boston: Little, Brown.

Thomas, Tony. 1974. *The Films of Gene Kelly: Song and Dance Man.* Secaucus, N.J.: Citadel Press.

Travers, Peter. 1989. "The Right Stuff." *Rolling Stone.* June 29: 27, 29.

Truffaut, François. 1978. "James Dean is Dead." In Leonard Mayhew, tr., *The Films in My Life.* New York: Simon & Schuster.

Truffaut, François, with Helen Scott. 1967. *Hitchcock.* New York: Simon & Schuster.

Wead, George and George Lellis. 1981. *Film: Form and Function.* Boston: Houghton, Mifflin.

Wollen, Peter. 1972. *Signs and Meaning in the Cinema.* Rev. ed. Bloomington: Indiana University Press.

Wood, Robin. 1965. *Hitchcock's Films.* New York: Tantivy Press.

Author

William Costanzo is professor of English at Westchester Community College, New York, where he has taught courses in writing, literature, and film for more than twenty years. His publications include *Double Exposure: Composing through Writing and Film* (1984), *The Electronic Text: Learning to Write, Read, and Reason with Computers* (1989), and more than forty articles and reviews. Since receiving his Ph.D. from Columbia University, he has received state and national awards for teaching and scholarship, and for designing educational software. Costanzo lectures widely on the educational uses of technology and has led workshops on media and English across the country. Within NCTE, he has served as director of the Commission on Media, chair of the Committee on Film Study in the English Language Arts, and chair of the Assembly on Media Arts. He currently serves on the Scholarly Advisory Board for The American Cinema Project, a new thirteen-part television series that examines the central concepts and themes in American feature filmmaking during the past sixty years. The series will air on PBS and be available as a television course in 1994.